T0013101

RETIREMENT 101

FROM **401(K) PLANS** AND **SOCIAL SECURITY BENEFITS** TO
ASSET MANAGEMENT AND **MEDICAL INSURANCE,** YOUR
COMPLETE GUIDE TO **PREPARING FOR THE FUTURE YOU WANT**

MICHELE CAGAN, CPA

Adams Media
New York London Toronto Sydney New Delhi

Adams Media
An Imprint of Simon & Schuster, Inc.
100 Technology Center Drive
Stoughton, MA 02072

First Adams Media hardcover edition December 2019

ADAMS MEDIA and colophon are trademarks of Simon & Schuster.

For information about special discounts for bulk purchases, please contact
Simon & Schuster Special Sales at 1-866-506-1949 or business@simonandschuster.com.

The Simon & Schuster Speakers Bureau can bring authors to your live event.
For more information or to book an event contact the Simon & Schuster Speakers Bureau at
1-866-248-3049 or visit our website at www.simonspeakers.com.

Manufactured in the United States of America

4 2023

Library of Congress Cataloging-in-Publication Data has been applied for.

ISBN 978-1-5072-1224-0
ISBN 978-1-5072-1225-7 (ebook)

CONTENTS

INTRODUCTION

If the word "retirement" makes you nervous, this is the book for you. Millions are concerned about retirement prospects. Many are worried about savings, about Social Security, and about rising healthcare costs.

The good news is that there a lot of things you can do to give yourself a more financially secure retirement. Once you figure out the kind of retirement you want, you can make a plan for it and start putting that plan into action.

What retirement really means is deciding what you want to do when you're ready to leave your full-time job. It means having the freedom to decide whether you want to work part time, go to school, travel, or just to kick back and relax. In order to achieve that freedom, you need to have enough cash to cover your expenses. Building up the biggest nest egg you possibly can gives you the most security and flexibility—and it's easier to do than you realize.

Throughout *Retirement 101,* you'll find things to do that will put you on firm financial ground for your retirement. You'll learn how to reduce and eventually eliminate debt. You'll plan how Social Security and savings fit into your ongoing financial picture. You'll find out how to manage your medical expenses while staying within your household budget.

Whether you're just starting to work on setting your retirement goals or are on the verge of wrapping up your career and leaving your job for good, this book will show you how to find and manage the money to fund your retirement. If you follow the recommendations in this book, you'll be able to set realistic retirement goals and meet them.

Taking action today and making a few simple changes can give you a more financially stable retirement. No matter your age, retirement goals, or the state of your finances, you'll be able to make a plan to get where you want to go. You'll start by assessing where you're at right now and then using that information to set a course for your goals. And this book will serve as a guidepost along the way.

Chapter 1

What Is Retirement?

Ask twenty people what retirement means, and you'll get twenty different answers, but you'll also hear some common themes. Retirement is about freedom and flexibility. It's defined by being able to stop trading time for money, but it doesn't mean you can't work if you want to. Retirement puts you in charge of your time. That's where retirement savings come in: To fund that phase of your life, you need to have access to a secure money supply.

THE TRUTH ABOUT "AVERAGE" RETIREMENT SAVINGS

Average Is Not the Goal

If you're trying to figure out if your retirement savings are "on track," you may have searched online to see what other people in your age group have saved. That information seems valuable after all—it gives you something to compare your savings with. But the "average" is not a good yardstick for a variety of reasons, not the least of which is that most Americans have underfunded their retirement accounts.

NOT REALLY AVERAGE

"Average" retirement savings calculations run into some pretty big snags, which is why they can look vastly different. For one thing, outliers (like supersavers or undersavers) can skew the numbers. Some averages include people who have no retirement savings at all, which also slants the results.

The other big factor: In general, we aren't saving enough. So using average savings as your benchmark could leave you with an underfunded retirement nest egg. Don't use the average as a goal. Consider it a measure that you want to surpass.

Average versus Median

Average retirement savings are calculated by adding up a specific number of account balances, then dividing that total dollar value by the count. For example, if a survey was looking for the average of

500 retirement accounts, it would total all their balances and then divide that sum by 500. If even one person had a balance that was very different than the others, it would knock the average out of line.

Looking at median savings may give a truer but still imperfect picture. The median offers the value that lies square in the middle, without any calculation. So if a survey looks at five hundred retirement accounts, and lists them from smallest to biggest, the median would be whichever account balance landed in the middle. With retirement savings, the average is always greater than the median, often two or three times as much as the median savings.

It Matters Where the Money Is

Average retirement savings numbers also overlook some very big questions, such as:

- Will the money be taxed in retirement?
- What will be the impact of account maintenance and investing fees?
- Will the money be invested and how?

Why does all that matter? Those three factors can each have a big impact on the future value of retirement savings, and the effect of all three combined can be monumental. For example, $50,000 in a Roth IRA that's invested in low-fee exchange-traded funds (ETFs) will be worth substantially more in retirement than $50,000 in a 401(k) that's invested in high-cost target date mutual funds (more on target date funds in Chapter 3). Roth IRA withdrawals are tax-free, while 401(k) withdrawals are subject to income taxes; that difference alone could change the true account value by tens of thousands of dollars at retirement time. High account maintenance fees and fund expenses eat away at earnings, reducing the compounding power of a portfolio. All in all, two retirement accounts with the same balance may not be equal.

A LOOK AT THE NUMBERS AND WHAT THEY MEAN

Even though "average retirement savings" numbers have limited usefulness and lots of flaws, they offer some insights into how Americans are preparing for the future. Different surveys will show different results, so if you're taking a look at the numbers, find out what's behind them (for example, a survey of 1,500 people gives a better picture than a survey of 75 people).

Baby Boomers

Baby boomers (people born between 1946 and 1964) are the closest generation to retirement age, but most are planning to keep working long past age sixty-five. Since defined contribution plans, like 401(k)s, showed up when most baby boomers were already well along in their careers, they didn't have the opportunity to start saving for retirement from the get-go. As a group, they started saving in earnest at around age thirty-five, giving them a shorter time frame for retirement savings to grow. Most (78 percent) are currently stashing money in retirement plans. Here's what their numbers look like:

- Median household retirement savings: $152,000
- Median retirement savings contribution rate: 10 percent of salary
- Proportion with *no* retirement savings: 9 percent

- Proportion with less than $50,000 saved: 16 percent
- Proportion with $250,000 or more saved: 39 percent

A Retirement Resource

The Transamerica Center for Retirement Studies offers one of the most detailed looks inside retirement in the US. All the numbers in this section are pulled from their 2018 report.

Generation X

Members of Generation X (born between 1965 and 1978) hit the workforce right around the same time that 401(k) plans appeared on the scene. They were really the first generation to have access to those plans for most of their careers, and most of them took full advantage. As financial setbacks hit, though, many used their retirement funds as backup savings, taking loans and early withdrawals to deal with current financial issues. That left many Gen X workers feeling insecure about their retirement nest eggs and struggling to catch up. Here's what their numbers look like:

- Median household retirement savings: $66,000
- Median retirement savings contribution rate: 8 percent of salary
- Proportion with *no* retirement savings: 10 percent
- Proportion with less than $50,000 saved: 27 percent
- Proportion with $250,000 or more saved: 24 percent

Millennials

Born between 1979 and 2000, Millennials take a more DIY approach to retirement. Most are starting out strong by participating in employer-sponsored retirement plans or creating their own. They take a very active approach to retirement planning and saving, and soak up information on what they can do to secure their financial futures. Here's what their numbers look like:

- Median household retirement savings: $23,000
- Median retirement savings contribution rate: 10 percent of salary
- Proportion with *no* retirement savings: 13 percent
- Proportion with less than $50,000 saved: 37 percent
- Proportion with $250,000 or more saved: 12 percent

WHAT DOES RETIREMENT LOOK LIKE?

A Glimpse of the Future

For most of us, retirement will last for twenty or thirty years. During that time, we'll move through three distinct phases. While the timing may be different (depending on things like your physical health and financial security), these stages are common to virtually everyone. Each phase calls for different financial moves and mindsets along with budget adjustments.

PHASE 1: JUST RETIRED

When you first retire (usually somewhere between ages sixty-two and seventy), your budget will undergo some notable changes. You'll have to adjust to the sudden lack of a steady paycheck, and make sure you take the steps necessary to be able to cover your monthly expenses. During this phase (depending on your age), you'll probably apply for Social Security and Medicare. As you get used to the changes in your immediate financial situation, you'll be able to craft your actual retirement budget (and see how close your estimates were) to make sure that you have what you need now without sabotaging your future needs.

Dramatic Shift in Income

On the income side, you'll stop getting regular paychecks from an employer (unless you have a pension plan). Depending on your age and available funds, you may apply for Social Security retirement benefits (details on how and when to do that are in Chapter 6). If you're at least age fifty-nine-and-a-half, you'll be able to start withdrawing funds from your retirement accounts without facing any tax penalties. You'll develop a withdrawal strategy and coordinate the timing of your incoming cash to make sure it meets your cash outflow needs.

Another big change: Once you stop getting a paycheck, you also stop prepaying federal and state (and maybe local) income taxes, which used to be taken out of your pay by your employer. Now, you will be responsible for making quarterly estimated tax payments to make up for that. Failing to make the payments, or not paying enough, could result in big tax penalties.

Loss of Employer Health Coverage

Another big change: You'll need to handle your own (and probably your family's) healthcare coverage. If you (and your spouse) are at least sixty-five years old, you can sign up for Medicare coverage. Otherwise, you'll need to self-fund your medical care, use COBRA coverage from your former employer (if it's available), or buy a plan on the healthcare marketplace.

COBRA (Consolidated Omnibus Budget Reconciliation Act)

If you've had health insurance through an employer, you may be able to get continued coverage with the same plan under the COBRA law. That coverage can last for up to eighteen months. You will be fully responsible for paying the premiums (which may be extremely expensive) but you will have the same exact health insurance you did before.

Spending

A lot of people move into this phase by traveling, taking up new hobbies, and spending money on things they've always wanted while they can enjoy them. The sudden surge of free time along with the realization that they're as young and healthy as they're ever going to be can set off spending sprees. There's nothing wrong with that as long as it's done with a plan and doesn't come at the expense of future financial security. This is also a time when many people consider relocating to live in lower-cost areas or to be closer to family.

PHASE 2: IN THE MIDDLE

Once you're in full-swing retirement (usually between ages seventy and seventy-eight), you'll be more used to managing your cash flows (both in and out). It's a time to take a critical look at your portfolio and revisit your asset allocation, the principle of investing in different types of assets (such as stocks, bonds, and real estate). During this phase, many people start to reduce their Phase 1 activities—they've traveled everywhere they wanted to go, for example. They may also start having new health concerns. These two factors can lead to a big shift in monthly expenses: Lower activity levels will reduce costs, while increasing healthcare needs will bring on different costs. In addition to some financial adjustments, this is the time to craft your estate plan and update (or put in place) legal documents.

Shifts in Cash Flow

This phase of retirement involves some "musts." You must start taking Social Security retirement benefits by age seventy. When you reach age seventy-and-a-half, you'll have to start taking required minimum distributions (RMDs) from some (or all) of your retirement accounts (excluding Roth IRAs). (You can find more information about RMDs in Chapter 5.)

It also often involves changes in the way you spend money. It's a more laid-back phase, where travel might be limited to visiting family, and activities take place closer to home. That can free up some money in your budget, allowing you to withdraw less cash (but not less than your RMDs) from your retirement nest egg.

Get Your Documents in Order

If you don't already have a will and other estate-planning documents in place, or if you haven't reviewed them in the past few years, this is the time to care of that. Get your estate plan in order to make sure that your assets are handled the way you want them to be once you pass away. While you're still of sound mind, designate a financial power of attorney to manage your money if you become unable to do it yourself. You'll also want to give someone your healthcare power of attorney to make medical decisions on your behalf if you need them to.

Power of Attorney

Granting someone "power of attorney" (POA) gives them the authority to act as you in specific situations. The powers include making decisions on your behalf, which may involve accessing all of your money and assets. That's why it's imperative that you only give a POA to someone you can trust 100 percent. While you're able to communicate, you can revoke a POA at any time.

PHASE 3: THE LATER YEARS

The later years of retirement may be marked by dramatic changes in your health and living situation. Medical spending tends to be the highest during this phase, and may put a significant strain on your budget.

Managing Medical Expenses

If you haven't had significant health issues before, you may not have paid too much attention to your Medicare plans. You can change that now, and find the right combination of Medicare coverage to meet your healthcare needs without depleting your nest egg. This may also be the time when you start to use long-term care insurance coverage (more on this critical topic in Chapter 5), if you need to move into an assisted living facility or require a home health aide. Finally, if you have any funds remaining in a health savings account (HSA), you can use them without increasing your tax bill at all.

Adding Financial Security

At this point in your retirement, it's best to focus your portfolio solely on preservation and income production. Reducing (even removing) risk will lower your investment returns, but it will also protect your nest egg from stock market losses and economy shocks. Shifting out of the stock market and into more stable investments like bonds will add another layer of financial security.

Another option: buying an immediate, fixed annuity. These are bare-bones annuities that act like pensions, supplying guaranteed periodic payments for life. You can choose from a variety of timelines (such as ten-year minimum, joint life for you and your spouse, or your lifespan) that fit your situation. (You can learn more about annuities in Chapter 8.)

DIFFERENT TAKES BY GENERATION

Baby Boomers, Millennials, and Gen-Xers

Retirement account balances aren't the only things that differ greatly based on generation. Different ages groups also have substantially different takes on almost every facet of retirement, from how long they plan to work, to how much they save, to how they describe retirement. Expectations are shifting dramatically as lifespan increases, as work trends toward self-employment and short-term gigs, and as drama surrounding potentially drastic changes to Social Security benefits increases. Not surprisingly, each generation has a different take on the many factors involved in retirement.

BABY BOOMERS

Known as the "trailblazer generation," baby boomers are creating their own rules for retirement, and are very much looking forward to it. Their savings took a beating during the devastating economic slump of the late 2000s, and they're still recovering. Most of them (around 63 percent) plan on working at their current jobs longer than originally expected, but they haven't figured out what they'll do if that doesn't work out, and they're forced to retire earlier.

Staying in the Work Force
The majority of baby boomers (69 percent) plan to (or are already) working beyond age sixty-five, mainly due to financial concerns.

Their vision includes taking a wading-in approach to retirement, where they'll start to work fewer hours or work in a different, less demanding capacity than their current full-time jobs. Many focus on learning new skills to improve their workplace value and boost their chances of finding work past age sixty-five.

Plus, about 26 percent of baby boomers say their ideal retirements include some form of work, whether that's going further in their current careers, switching tracks toward an "encore" career, or starting their own companies.

For Fun

Outside of continuing work, baby boomers plan to enjoy active retirements. Their top-rated retirement dreams include:

- Traveling
- Spending time with family and friends
- Pursuing hobbies
- Volunteering

To that end, baby boomers are very focused on health, and consistently take part in health-related activities like exercise, eating healthfully, and managing stress.

Common Fears

Despite different views on retirement, some fears are common across the generations. The biggest fears include financial insecurity, outliving their money, declining health (especially cognitive decline), and social isolation.

GENERATION X

Despite the fact that 77 percent of Gen-Xers are actively saving for retirement, as a group they don't feel confident that they'll have enough money to support themselves once they retire. In fact, fewer than 15 percent feel "very confident" that they'll be able to retire completely and live comfortably. Many have a dim view of retirement, and associate it with ill health and severe budget cuts. Luckily, this generation still has some time on their side to build up bigger nest eggs and greater financial security.

Trying to Catch Up

The Great Recession derailed members of Generation X just as they were finally feeling flush. The sudden drop in portfolio and home values took a huge toll on their financial situations. That's why it's not surprising that a large proportion (more than 30 percent) of Gen-Xers have pulled money out of their retirement savings, leaving a gaping hole in their future finances. In fact, 25 percent of Gen X members have less than $5,000 in retirement savings.

This generation also struggles with debt (some still lingering from the recession), mainly in the form of large credit card balances. On top of all that, about a third of Gen-Xers are caring for their parents or other older family members, right as their children are hitting college age.

Despite these setbacks, many Gen-Xers are ramping up savings both inside and outside of employer plans to help fund their retirement dreams, even if it will take them a little longer to get there.

More Than a Paycheck

Most Gen-Xers plan on working through retirement in one way or another. While income is a key factor in that choice, it's not the only one. Many feel that continued work will keep them mentally and socially active. Rather than taking a traditional view of retirement, they plan to incorporate work into their lives for as long as possible.

Outside of work, most members of Generation X hope to travel during their retirement. Many also plan to pursue new hobbies and spend more time doing the things they love. Their work/life balance will gradually shift toward more life and less work.

Working Without a Plan

Having a thorough, written plan is a key component of building a sufficient retirement nest egg. Most members of Generation X don't have such a plan in place; in fact, only about 14 percent report having written strategic retirement plans.

MILLENNIALS

Millennials are taking a proactive approach to retirement savings, which puts them in a great position to retire with substantial nest eggs. They expect to live long (age 100 or older) and support themselves, as most don't trust that Social Security will be around by the time they retire. While they are getting an early start, most don't feel confident about making the right investment choices to reach their retirement goals.

Dancing with Debt

Among the three generations, millennials have more debt. This makes sense because they've been in the workforce for less time, they've amassed more credit card debt, and they haven't had as much time to pay off student loans. Unfortunately, many (around 36 percent) have turned to 401(k) loans to pay down debt, which can take a long-term toll on retirement savings.

Taking Advantage of Information

Most millennials take a DIY approach to retirement, using technology to automate, track, and revise their contributions. They're also hungry for advice on how to reach their retirement goals, from making realistic estimates about future needs to developing the most productive portfolios. Approximately 72 percent feel like "they don't know as much as they should" about managing their retirement funds. Nearly 40 percent turn to professional financial advisors, according to the Transamerica Center for Retirement Studies.

Strong Savers

That Transamerica report also reveals that 71 percent of millennials already contribute to retirement plans, both inside and outside of the workplace. On average, they put 10 percent of their salaries into those plans. Already, about 12 percent of millennials have built up retirement savings of at least $250,000.

FUTURE CHANGES AND CHALLENGES

Gaze Into My Crystal Ball

From insecurity about Social Security to rapidly changing technologies, the future holds many uncertainties and prospects for retirees. Some of these seem fairly predictable, so you can plan around them, like making sure you won't have to rely on Social Security to pay the rent. Others you might never see coming, like a robot butler serving your morning coffee with a side of portfolio adjustment. The key to weathering any of these future surprises is a solid nest egg and flexible planning; armed with those, you'll be able to adapt to whatever the future brings.

POTENTIAL CHANGES TO SOCIAL SECURITY AND MEDICARE

No matter how you look at it, the Social Security and Medicare programs are both in precarious financial positions. Potential solutions almost always involve cutting benefits in one way or another along with FICA (payroll) tax hikes. That means you could be paying in more during your working years, and receiving less (or later) money after you retire—not an ideal situation.

Social Security Alone Won't Cover It

With the Social Security trust fund set to run out of money sometime in the mid-2030s (possibly as soon as 2034), changes to the system are inevitable. Possible fixes to the system include raising the full retirement age, reducing retirement benefits, and increasing Social Security taxes. The most likely of those is a cut in benefits, which would pay future retirees around 75 percent of what they'd get today.

Since nearly one-third of workers expect Social Security to be their primary source of income in retirement, those cuts could be devastating. Considering that the average full monthly Social Security retirement benefit ($1,461 in 2019) can barely cover monthly living expenses as it is, potential cuts shift even more burden onto us. That said, Social Security benefits will remain a reliable source of income for retirees for decades to come—it just won't provide enough to live on.

Medicare Modifications

According to the Centers for Medicare and Medicaid Services (CMS at www.cms.gov), Medicare covers nearly 60 million beneficiaries and spends around $741 billion (as of 2018), more than it collects in income. Based on those numbers, the trustees estimate the Medicare trust fund will run dry by 2026. Between recent tax changes, a growing proportion of older adults, and skyrocketing healthcare costs, the system may need to make some drastic modifications to stay afloat.

The Impact on Care and Costs

While some proposed changes to Medicare seem to aim at reducing waste and fraud, they could impact quality of patient care and limit care choices. Future retirees also face the possibility of increased Medicare premiums, deductibles, and copays, which could add substantially to their healthcare costs.

TAKING ADVANTAGE OF FUTURE TECH

Driverless cars, smart homes, and biometrics are among the many new developing technologies that will affect both retirement and retirement savings. From wearable monitors that track your health 24/7 to robot pets that offer companionship and anxiety reduction (but never pee on the floor), new products geared toward seniors are hitting the market in record numbers. Two of the biggest trends (smart homes and robo-advisors) already make life easier for millions of people.

Personalized Homes

Retirement often comes with downsizing, especially when it comes to living quarters. Not only will retirees' homes be smaller, they'll also cater to your specific needs. Flexible rooms and furnishings will make it easier to age in place; for example, shifting walls or shelving will let you easily transition should a wheelchair become necessary.

More Sensitive Robo-Advisors

Robo-advisors completely automate the investing process. These online programs use complex algorithms to optimize investment portfolios. Already millions of people use robo-advisors to manage and rebalance their portfolios every day. As the technology gets more sophisticated, it may become more predictive, giving you a better chance of avoiding losses. Robo-advisors may begin to more actively manage portfolios with up-to-the-nanosecond access to market activity. Straightforward investing platforms may morph into sophisticated retirement planning and wealth management strategies. For people who embrace the robo-style, saving and investing for retirement could take nothing more than answering a few questions once a year.

Chapter 2

When Can You Afford to Retire?

Will you be able to retire by age sixty-five or be stuck working past age seventy? There's not a simple answer to that question; in fact, there are multiple answers. Two people with the exact same amount of retirement savings today could achieve financial independence years or even decades apart. A multitude of factors affect *your* answer to that question, from your investment choices to your monthly expenses to physical health. When you know which factors matter more and how to adjust them in your favor, you'll have more control over your retirement age.

PLAN FOR RETIREMENT AT ANY AGE

Are You On Track?

It's frustrating trying to figure out whether or not you're on track for a financially comfortable retirement. With so many different models you could use and dozens of variables to consider, it's easy to get overwhelmed and put it off. The truth is, it's not as difficult or discouraging as it seems—but it does involve a chunk of time and a little math. Then, you'll do some periodic quick checks to make sure you stay on the right track.

KNOW YOUR LIFE EXPECTANCY

One of the biggest question surrounding retirement savings is "How long do I need the money to last?" Unfortunately, there's no definitive answer, but there are specific factors you can take into account to come up with a realistic estimate. That expected longevity will play an important part in your retirement plan projections. It will affect how much money you need overall, your safe withdrawal rate, and the best way to structure your retirement portfolio.

Start with the Average

According to the Centers for Disease Control and Prevention (CDC), the average overall life expectancy in the US is 78.6 years. That number changes a little when you break it out by gender: The average lifespan for men is 76.1 and for women is 81.1.

The numbers still look different if you look at life expectancy after age sixty-five. Overall, that number is 19.5 years; so someone who's sixty-five now can expect to live until age eighty-four and a half. Gender makes a difference here too. Women age sixty-five and older have a life expectancy of 20.6 years, and men can expect an average 18.1 additional years.

Try a Life Expectancy Calculator

There are dozens of life expectancy calculators online that will give you a more tailored response than the CDC averages. They tend to ask a lot of the same questions (current age, blood pressure, exercise, smoking, etc.) but each has their own little twist. Since they're free, you can try as many as you want to get a more complete picture of your life expectancy.

Here are some calculators (usually located in the "tools" menu) that aren't super invasive and don't make you hand over your email address:

- How Long Will I Live? by Blueprint Income (www.blueprintincome.com)
- Life Expectancy Calculator by Bankrate (www.bankrate.com)
- Life Span Calculator by Northwestern Mutual Life Insurance Company (www.northwesternmutual.com)
- Life Expectancy Calculator by John Hancock Life Insurance Company (www.johnhancockinsurance.com)

KNOW YOUR NEST EGG TARGET

You'll hear numbers like $500,000 or $1,000,000 thrown around a lot in the retirement planning world. Instead of going with guesswork, take some time to come up with a number that works for your personal situation. A whole host of variables will factor into your retirement needs, from where you'll live, to whether you're supporting your children or parents, to the general state of your health. Figuring out your target nest egg will take a little time and some math. Once you have that, you can create a savings and investment plan that will get you there in plenty of time.

Make a Written Plan

Most people don't have written retirement plans, and that can make it harder to keep retirement savings on track. Putting a plan in writing does the following:

- Clarifies your goals and expectations
- Lets you know when you hit benchmarks
- Forces you to think about potential obstacles
- Involves some tax and estate planning
- Helps you refine your investment strategies
- Lets you come up with backup plans before you need them

If you're not sure how to put all this together, think about consulting a fee-based financial advisor. They can help you create a flexible plan with a realistic retirement savings goal.

Set Your Target

To set your target nest egg, think about how much money you'll need to spend every year in retirement. Your expenses may be pretty close to the same or dramatically different (if you move to a different area, for example). Either way, you'll need enough money to cover taxes and your basic known living expenses: housing, food, transportation, healthcare premiums, etc. Plus, you'll need money available to cover the fun stuff like dining out, travel, and entertainment. Adding all of that together will give you a rough idea of the annual "salary" you'll need in retirement. Take that result and multiply it by 25 or 30 (years) to come up with a baseline estimate of the money you'll need to stockpile in order to afford a comfortable retirement.

Remember, this looks only at the expense side of your equation and doesn't account for guaranteed income (such as Social Security retirement benefits) or strong investment returns.

Climate Change and Retirement Savings

Climate change appears to have a double-sided direct effect on retirement savings. On one side, younger generations have a more "why bother?" approach to savings, as they expect catastrophic climate consequences in their lifetimes. On the other side, few corporations and investment funds have changed their strategies or outlooks to respond to climate change, leading to inevitable financial losses that will directly impact many people's retirement nest eggs through plummeting share prices and nonexistent dividends.

Don't Get Sidetracked by Fear

Many conversations about retirement end up being discussions about fears and concerns. People are afraid they'll outlive their money and be unable to afford their family's basic needs. They worry about ending up in long-term care that forces them into bankruptcy. Fear of loss, isolation, declining health, and poverty colors what should be a golden, stress-free (or at least low-stress) time of life. Worrying about trying to save $1,000,000 can be unnerving and make you feel like there's no point in even trying. That negativity trap can convince you that you'll never be able to save enough or that a comfortable retirement is hopeless.

Focusing on those scary what-ifs is paralyzing. Try to reframe the conversation to be about what a better retirement would look like. Look at the things you can start doing now to help counter those what-ifs. For example, if your biggest fear is going broke paying for a nursing home, look into long-term care insurance options, or start self-insuring by building up a sizeable HSA (health savings account). Address those fears, and turn them around before they disrupt your dream retirement.

WHEN ARE YOUR SAVINGS ENOUGH?

Are We There Yet?

You can't tell if you're saving "enough" if you don't have a goal in mind. The first step in saving for retirement is figuring out how much money you'll need. That starts with taking a look at your current budget and lifestyle, and considering which things are likely to change once you retire. Think about whether you'll be spending more or less money every month, and which expenses might increase. Once you have an idea of your expected spending, shift gears and take a look at your current savings and your retirement time frame. This combination of factors will dictate how much you need to save now and moving forward.

HOW MUCH *MORE* DO YOU NEED?

Once you know your nest egg goal, you can figure out how much more you need to save. That number starts with a basic retirement budget: your total expected monthly expenses, your guaranteed income (such as existing pensions and Social Security benefits), and the amount you'll need to make up the coverage difference each month. The total expenses minus the guaranteed income equals the coverage difference.

Say your expected monthly expenses come to $3,500 per month and your guaranteed income sources will be $2,200 (both your and your spouse's Social Security). The coverage difference will be $1,300 per month, or $15,600 per year. If you plan to be retired for twenty-five years, you would need a total retirement nest egg of at least $390,000 ($15,600 × 25). This super-simplified model doesn't take into account things like inflation, investment earnings (or losses), taxes, and other variables. But it will give you an idea of what size nest egg you'll need.

Help from the IRS? *Yes!*

The US Internal Revenue Service (IRS) has a special program called Tax Counseling for the Elderly (TCE). The program offers free year-round tax counseling and tax return preparation for adults aged sixty and older. These tax preparers specialize in pension and retirement issues, and help you figure out estimated tax payments. Find out more at www.irs.gov.

THE DIFFERENCE BETWEEN INCOME AND CASH FLOW

The terms "income" and "cash flow" are often used interchangeably, especially when talking about retirement. They aren't the same, though, and that can trip you up. In retirement, cash flow becomes more important than income.

Everyone understands income: money you earn from a job or business, investment earnings (like interest and dividends), Social Security benefits, and so on. Income shows up every year on your tax return, so it's familiar. Cash flow describes when and how money moves in and out. When you pay expenses, cash is flowing out; when you receive income or take withdrawals from retirement and other accounts, cash is flowing in. Those two numbers are almost never equal.

Retirement Cash Flow Comes from Earnings and Principal

A large part of retirement income isn't technically income; it's money pulled from savings that's a combination of investment earnings (income) and principal (the money you've already saved).

When you withdraw principal, it reduces the future earnings (there's less money available to earn interest or dividends), and that can impact your cash flow (the amount of money available to withdraw). You'll (typically) need to withdraw more than you earn. By focusing on the amount you'll need to withdraw every month to cover your expenses, you'll have a better sense of how to make your retirement nest egg last.

Time Your Cash Flow

In addition to your standard monthly expenses, there may be some big purchases that you know will be coming up. This may include things like a car (which usually needs to be replaced about every ten years or so) or a major home repair. By mapping out those large expenditures on a timeline, you can see when you'll need the extra cash flow well in advance. For example, if you know you'll need a new car in seven years, you can invest in a bond or open a CD that will mature in seven years, matching up your cash inflows and outflows.

TAKE ADVANTAGE OF FREE ONLINE CALCULATORS

If you Google "retirement calculators," you'll get more hits than you could ever want to go through. These online tools help you do the hard math behind retirement savings and earnings calculations, and they let you know whether you're on track for a comfortable retirement. They run the gamut from simple snapshots to complex reports, and it'll be tough to find two that serve up the exact same answers (but they'll usually be in the same range).

The best retirement calculators are easy to use, offer the flexibility to change variables (rather than making you accept their programmed averages), and deliver clear results. They'll let you know if your current savings and earnings trajectory should be able to cover the annual withdrawals you expect to make.

Reliable Results

No retirement calculator is perfect; they're not supposed to be. Good ones will supply realistic, reliable outcomes based on the variables you enter so you can see whether your savings are on track. Some are offered by brokerage firms, but you typically don't need to have an account with them to use the online tools or apps. Here are some solid, basic retirement calculators:

- MaxiFi (www.maxifiplanner.com)
- Fidelity Retirement Score (www.fidelity.com)
- T. Rowe Price Retirement Income Calculator (www.troweprice.com)
- MarketWatch Retirement Calculator (www.marketwatch.com)

Use Secure Sites

Because you'll be entering at least some level of personal financial information into whichever online calculator you choose, make sure to use only secure websites on secure Wi-Fi. On the website side, input information only on sites with "https" in the address and a padlock icon.

That indicates that the site has the encryption security protocol, Secure Sockets Layer (SSL), which delivers a secure, encrypted link between your computer and their website. This means the information you're sending—your personal financial information—is private and secure.

On the Wi-Fi side, *never* use public Wi-Fi when you're dealing with personal information of any kind, especially financial information. Public Wi-Fi is readily accessible, and that openness makes it very easy for snoops and thieves to "see" your information. Plus, hackers may set themselves up as middlemen in between you and the public Wi-Fi, so everything you do gets routed through them first.

Check In with Your Financial Professional

If you have an existing relationship with a financial professional, such as your Certified Public Accountant (CPA), they may run the numbers for you as part of their service; all you have to do is ask. Financial professionals have access to more robust planning models than the rest of us. Many of them offer free retirement checkup services for their clients (though more involved planning sessions will normally come at a cost). Free check-ins can range from 401(k) rebalancing, to "am I on track?" analyses, to nest-egg target estimates. If your financial professional offers a free retirement checkup, take advantage of it every year.

CHANGE THE VARIABLES

Once you've done a few rounds of calculations using the most likely scenarios, it's time to switch things up. Now, you'll want to stress-test your plans to see what would happen in some what-if situations.

Some of the varying factors include:

- Annual withdrawals
- Time horizon
- Projected investment returns
- Portfolio allocation
- Size of nest egg
- Inflation

You may also want to add variables that many basic online retirement calculators don't track, such as the impact of taxes, sudden spending needs (such as medical costs), or a major life change (such as divorce or the death of a spouse).

Understand Sequence Risk

When you're putting money into your retirement account, the order of returns doesn't matter. Over the long haul, you could have light earnings some years (say, 3 percent or 4 percent), super earnings in other years (8 percent to 12 percent, for example), and sustain losses in still other years; but the average returns over that whole period would still be positive and your nest egg would grow. Because there's plenty of time, the sequence of those returns doesn't matter at all, just the end result.

Sequence matters enormously once you stop contributing and start withdrawing. Now, the order of the returns can completely make or break your nest egg, regardless of their average. For example, if your first few years of retirement coincide with negative market returns, your nest egg never has the chance to recover from those losses even if the market recovery is strong. So, you could have the exact same size of nest egg, allocations, and diversification as another person who retired a few years before or after you did, and wind up with a totally different outcome based solely on timing and due to sequence risk.

Monte Carlo Simulations Stress-Test Your Plan

Monte Carlo simulations are mathematical forecasting models designed to predict the probability of various outcomes. It uses different possibilities to account for uncertainties, and when it comes to retirement forecasting, there are a lot of unpredictable factors at play. A Monte Carlo model calculates the results many times, substituting different values for the uncertainties to see what would happen in each circumstance.

Running Monte Carlo simulations is critical for realistic retirement planning for a number of reasons, but mainly because there's no way to know the level of returns your retirement portfolio will earn. Plus, there's no way to know the state that the markets or the general economy will be in after you've retired. This type of modeling helps you see the effects of several different scenarios so you can make adjustments to your strategy before it's too late.

Note: Monte Carlo simulations are better than static retirement calculators, but they aren't perfect. Most don't account for sequence risk, and none of them guarantee accurate results. They're just tools to help stress-test your portfolio and stay on track for a comfortable retirement.

Flexible Online Planning Tools

Many online retirement calculators are one-note tools, but there are some planning tools that consider many more variables and use some variation of the Monte Carlo method. These programs run the numbers to come up with a probability factor, the likelihood that your retirement plan will deliver the income you expect to need. For example, if you think you'll need $65,000 a year in retirement, the program will return the probability of that happening based on the information you input.

You can test your plan using free online tools (you may have to set up an account, but there's no fee to use the calculator), such as:

- Flexible Retirement Planner (www.flexibleretirementplanner.com)
- FIRECalc (www.firecalc.com)
- Optimal Retirement Planner (www.i-orp.com)

These tools ask for quite a bit of information, so expect to spend a good amount of time with them, especially if you want to run a few different scenarios.

TAKE A DEEP LOOK AT YOUR FINANCES

Money under a Microscope

The first step in making a financial plan is to know—really know—your current financial situation. A lot of people shy away from this step because they don't want to see "how bad things really are." No matter what the situation is, there are things you can do to improve it. If you're in great financial shape, you can take your finances to the next level. If your finances need some work, you'll know how to approach that.

MONTHLY EXPENSES MATTER MOST

Retirement finances are all about cash flow, making sure you have enough money available coming in to cover all the money you need to pay out. By minimizing your core monthly expenses—the absolutely necessary expenses you can't skip—you give yourself more financial flexibility. Basically, there are two ways to break down expenses: fixed and variable, or needs and wants.

Fixed expenses are the same every month and include things like rent or mortgage payments, minimum credit card payments, other loan payments, phone service, insurance, and subscriptions. Variable expenses fluctuate based on circumstance and include things like electric bills, food, gasoline, entertainment, clothes, and gifts.

Needs include only the things you cannot live without—food, clothing, shelter, medical care, and transportation. Wants include higher-end versions of needs (for example, you need food but you don't need takeout) and things that you could live without (even if you don't want to), such as streaming service, throw pillows, and massages.

Don't Forget Periodic Expenses

Not every expense gets paid monthly, but even occasional fixed expenses should factor into your monthly budget. To find these often-overlooked budget busters, look through an entire year's worth of bank and credit card statements. When you come across a periodic expense (such as property tax payments), divide it up into a monthly expense and add it to the list.

KNOW YOUR NET WORTH

Understanding your current financial situation starts with figuring out your net worth. That value marks the cornerstone of your financial life. By knowing your net worth, you'll be better able to make key financial decisions to further your retirement savings goals. It lets you know what shape your finances are in today, and gives you a clear starting point for measuring your progress in achieving your goals.

Net Worth Math

The basic formula for calculating net worth is simple: Assets – Liabilities = Net Worth. Gathering up all the information you need to get to the equation will take a little bit of your time.

Net worth starts with your assets, basically everything that you own. Next, it removes your liabilities, which is all the money you owe.

If your total assets are greater than your total liabilities, you have a positive net worth. If it's the other way around, and you owe more than you own (at least for right now), your net worth is negative. Whatever the result, it's better to know it and to start taking actions to increase it.

Net Worth by the Numbers

According to the most recent Federal Reserve Survey of Consumer Finances, Americans' overall median household net worth is $97,300. Broken out by age group, the numbers look very different. As you'd expect, the numbers get bigger as age increases. The median net worth of the under-thirty-five crowd is $11,100, compared to $264,800 for people age seventy-five and older.

Negative Isn't Unusual

It's perfectly normal to have a negative net worth if you've been out of the work force or are just starting out in it. For example, if you're fresh out of school and packing some student loans, renting an apartment, and starting your first job, it would be weird if you didn't have a negative net worth. Another situation where negative net worth is normal: right after a divorce, when assets get sold or split, and liabilities (like lawyer's bills) creep up.

Don't let a negative net worth discourage you—it's just a temporary situation, and it still gives you a yardstick for measuring your progress.

IMPROVE YOUR NET WORTH

No matter what your net worth is, you can make it better. Going into retirement with a strong net worth can make the difference between financial security and running out of money. Steps you take today to improve your financial position will have a lasting, positive effect on your financial future.

There are two ways to affect your net worth: Increase your assets or decrease your liabilities. Your current financial situation will dictate which side of the equation to focus more of your attention on.

Add to Your Assets

To boost your net worth, you can build up your assets in different ways by doing the following:

- **Increase your work-related income:** Whether you ask for a raise, move to a higher-paying job, or take on a side gig, bringing in more money gives you the chance to build up your assets.
- **Build savings:** When you have savings, your money will start earning its own money in the form of interest; plus, you won't have to rely on credit cards and loans to cover unexpected expenses (which means you won't have to *pay* interest).
- **Invest more:** Whether you do it inside or outside of a retirement account, investing is one of the best ways to increase your net worth; if you're unsure of where to put your money, start with low-fee broad market funds and expand outward from there.

Decreasing Debt

If you don't have much in the way of assets but are carrying student loans and credit card debt, work on reducing your debt load. Not only will you improve your net worth, you'll also get to keep more of your money going forward because lower debt balances mean reduced interest charges. Dealing with debt can be disheartening, especially when it feels like there's no way out. Don't look at the big picture. Start by focusing only on your smallest debt and paying as much extra as you can (even if it's only a few dollars). Do your best to not take on any additional debt; avoiding new debt counts as a win. Sticking with these steps (as much as you can) will help you decrease your debt and increase your net worth.

KNOW YOUR CASH FLOW

Once you've retired, your cash will flow differently, especially if you were an employee with a regular paycheck. You'll have to make a lot of decisions about your incoming cash, and the right choices will make sure you don't fall short (at least not for expected expenses). Those decisions will involve both dollar amounts and timing, some of which you'll have more control over than others. For example, you can take any amount of money out of your 401(k) at any time once you turn age fifty-nine-and-a-half, but you can't start receiving fixed-payment Social Security retirement benefits until you're sixty-two.

Guaranteed Cash Flow

Guaranteed payments will be the cornerstone of your retirement income. This includes Social Security retirement benefits, employer pensions, annuities, and any other money that you will receive—without fail—every month. Less common guaranteed payments figure in here, too, and may include things like alimony, legal settlements, and lottery winnings. Some of these payments are guaranteed for life, others come with conditions (such as remaining unmarried) or end dates. When you do your cash flow planning, make sure you only include unconditional guaranteed payments, even those with end dates; just remember to change your income level when those payments are set to stop.

Timing Matters

Timing is one of the most important facets of cash flow management. You need your cash inflows to show up before it's time to make expense payments, or you risk running short and having to make unplanned cutbacks or getting hit with late payment fees, penalties, and interest.

There are two levels of timing for retirement cash flows: the year you expect them to start (for example, when you'll start taking Social Security retirement benefits) and when you'll actually receive cash in your bank accounts every month.

Start by taking a look at the timing of your expenses, including those that aren't a regular part of your budget, such as a vacation or a major home repair. Make a cash outflow timeline so you can match up your future expected income streams.

GET RID OF DEBT

Toss the Financial Albatross

Debt is one of the biggest obstacles to a stress-free retirement. It keeps your fixed expenses high, forcing you to withdraw more of your money every month. Plus, the interest you're paying is like negative investment earnings that you'll never recover. Retiring with debt—especially high-rate credit card debt—is one of the most common regrets among retirees. In fact, 40 percent of retirees (according to the Transamerica Center for Retirement Studies) prioritize paying debt, ranking it just as high as being able to cover basic living expenses. Taking steps to pay down as much debt as possible before retirement is a double win: It will remove a major stressor and reduce the amount of interest you pay out over your lifetime.

CREDIT CARD DEBT

Since credit card debt carries high interest rates, it can take years—even decades—to pay off that debt, and that's if you always pay at least the minimum payment on time. Skip a month or pay late and you'll get hit with fees (that get added to your balance) and higher penalty interest rates, making your debt even harder to pay down.

Focus On the Highest-Interest Debt

The fastest way to ditch credit card debt is to stop using the card with the highest interest rate and focus on paying it off. Tackling this first will save you the most money on interest. The less interest you're paying to the credit card company, the more you'll have available to pay off debt and increase your net worth. You'll find the interest rates right on your credit card statements.

Pay Strategically

First rule of paying off credit cards: Never pay late. Second rule: Always pay more than the minimum payment (even $5 more). Third rule: Pay early.

Because of the way credit card interest is charged, you'll actually save money by making your payment as soon as you get the statement rather than near or on the due date. If you can't swing that due to cash flow issues, make two (or more) payments every month, starting as soon as possible. They charge interest on the average daily balance, so reducing your balance earlier in the month also reduces the average daily balance. By lowering the interest charge, more of your next payment will go toward principal, accelerating your paydown rate.

Drowning in Debt

Americans are drowning in credit card debt. According to the Federal Reserve, we owe a grand total of $1.064 *trillion*, and the average household credit card debt is $8,339 (as of April 2019). Looking a little closer, the average credit debt by person (instead of household) is $5,839 (according to www.creditdonkey.com). That average cranks up to $7,527 for people who carry a balance.

STUDENT LOANS

For adults over age sixty, student loan debt has been on the rise. According to the Consumer Financial Protection Bureau (CFPB), the number of older adult borrowers in this category increased by more than 20 percent between 2012 and 2017. Not surprisingly, most of those borrowers (73 percent) took on the new debt for children and grandchildren, rather than for themselves. On average, retirees owe about $20,000 in student loans. Overall, according to *Forbes*, adults aged sixty to sixty-nine owe a collective $85.4 billion of student loan debt.

Cosigners Are 100 Percent Responsible

Many people don't realize that cosigning for a loan makes them 100 percent responsible for the loan payments if the other borrower doesn't make payments. If you cosign on a student loan for someone else, you will be on the hook if that person defaults. Since there's no collateral backing the loan, there's nothing for the lender to repossess, so the only way they can get their money back is by coming after you as the cosigner. This very common situation forces older adults to either stop saving for retirement or raid their retirement savings to make loan payments.

Consequences of Default

According to the CFPB, around 40 percent of people who are at least sixty-five years old and have federal student loan debt are in default (have stopped making payments). If you're in that position, be aware that you could be facing some extra financial consequences.

If your debt includes federal student loans, the government can garnish (take) up to 15 percent of your Social Security retirement benefits every month. They can also seize your federal income tax refunds. Plus, student loans are practically impossible to give rid of through bankruptcy, meaning even if you declare bankruptcy the student loans still have to be paid.

What You Can Do

If you haven't yet retired, do whatever you can to pay off your student loans. Federal loan programs offer a wide variety of income-based payment plans that can at least keep your loan balance from getting bigger. When you don't make payments, you're still charged interest, and that gets added to your loan balance; this is one of those times that the power of compounding works against you. Even if you're already in default, you can "rehabilitate" your loan status and qualify for a payment plan.

If you're already retired and are unable to cover your living expenses and outstanding student loan payments, you may also be able to change the payment plan to one you can afford. Consider consolidating (not refinancing) your federal student loans to make it easier to avoid future default. Visit https://studentaid.ed.gov to see if one of their repayment plans fits your situation.

THE MORTGAGE

Most people's biggest fixed expense is their monthly mortgage payment. It usually comes with the lowest interest rate of their total debt picture, putting it last on the debt paydown list. Most mortgages allow prepayments; check your loan to see if there's any prepayment penalty in place before you start paying extra.

There are two easy ways to make extra payments on your mortgage. You can just add money to your monthly payment (like rounding a $1,526 payment up to $1,600) and designate it as extra principal. You can make an extra, separate payment and instruct the lender to apply it to principal. The key here: Make sure the lender applies your payment to principal. Most lenders will have instructions on their websites to tell you how to label the payment properly.

If the interest rate on your mortgage is higher than current interest rates, consider refinancing to lower your rate, especially if you have a strong credit score. Not only will you almost always get better rates with a shorter loan term, you'll also stay on track to pay it off completely. Before you refinance, though, run the numbers through a refinancing calculator to make sure you'll save money by doing it. You can find good refinancing calculators online at *NerdWallet* (www.nerdwallet.com) and *Zillow* (www.zillow.com). If it makes sense, shop around for the best combination of lower rate and low closing costs. Two things not to do here: Don't take cash out, and don't extend your loan term.

PREPARE FOR CHANGING EXPENSES

Curveballs Ahead

When you're about five years out from retirement, it's time to create a thorough retirement budget. This will offer you a realistic picture of how much money you'll need every month. By projecting that out with steady inflation increases over your estimated life expectancy, you'll be able to see how close your current savings are to being able to meet your needs. If you're on track, great; if not, you still have time to ramp up savings and make other changes that will help you have a more financially secure retirement.

PREPARE FOR HEALTHCARE

No matter how healthy you are right now, at some point your healthcare costs will increase. That's partly because virtually everyone uses more healthcare services as they age, and partly because medical expenses can increase faster than inflation.

This is one budget area that most people are unprepared for. They tend to overestimate how much Medicare will cover and underestimate their eventual medical needs.

Build Up Your HSA Balance

An HSA (health savings account) serves as one of the best weapons in your retirement arsenal. All the contributions you make to the HSA are tax deductible (or pre-tax if those contributions are made directly through your paycheck). The money in the account grows tax-deferred, meaning you don't pay any taxes on the earnings while they remain inside the account. Best of all, if you use the money to pay for medical expenses, you never have to pay tax on it—not one penny.

Benefits Work for Everyone

Since everyone will need some kind of healthcare at some point, the triple tax benefits of HSAs work for everyone. If it turns out you need the money for something other than healthcare costs, once you turn sixty-five, you can use that money for anything you want but you will have to pay regular income taxes on withdrawals (though you will avoid tax penalties).

While the money builds up inside your HSA, you can invest it in low-cost exchange-traded funds or mutual funds. This gives your account the best chance for growth. That strategy works best for people who don't need to use the HSA to cover current medical expenses.

Safeguard Your Health

You control (at least partially) the nonfinancial side of the health-care equation. There are things you can do to improve your current and future health outlook. Virtually every doctor will tell you to stop smoking, eat better, and exercise; all of those will keep you healthier and ward off a wide variety of chronic conditions. If you do have a chronic condition (such as high blood pressure or diabetes), do your best to get it under control as early as possible to limit its damage potential. The more you do to improve your overall health now, the better your chances of a healthier (and less expensive) retirement.

PLAN FOR THE UNEXPECTED

Whether you're preparing for retirement or you're living on a fixed income, unexpected changes in your financial situation can have a dramatic impact on your budget and your savings. Some of the most common curveballs include:

- Reduced income, due to job loss, end of annuity payments, or other causes
- Emergency spending, due to a flood or a car accident, for example
- Lasting cost increases, such as higher insurance premiums or raised rent
- Divorce, which is becoming increasingly common for adults age fifty and older

Although you can't predict the future, you can plan for an unspecified, unexpected event or two. Keep your emergency savings funded even after retirement. If you don't have emergency savings, work on building it up. Remember, this is savings, so lock this money away somewhere safe; don't invest it.

Chapter 3

How to Build a Big Retirement Nest Egg

It can be hard to find "extra" money to contribute to retirement savings, but you have to—and you have to start right now. Consider this: If you're having a hard time finding the money now, imagine how much harder it will be when you're seventy or eighty years old. Even if you can only contribute a few hundred dollars a year, that's better than saving nothing. Every dollar you sock away now has the potential to grow into thousands of dollars over time—if it has enough time to grow.

START EARLY, KEEP SAVING

Time Is on Your Side

When retirement feels very far away, it's hard to get motivated to start saving, but when you're young is the absolute best time to start. You have the most possible time on your side, which means you can contribute less money but still finish with more money, thanks to the power of compounding interest (how your money earns its own money).

Motivate yourself to save by visualizing yourself in the future. Remember that every dollar you save now will go toward supporting you and your financial security. It can be hard to prioritize the distant future when you're working to support yourself (and maybe your family) and pay off debt today, but it's 100 percent worth it.

AUTOMATE TO STAY ON TRACK

The easiest way to save money is to do it without thinking. By setting up automatic contributions to a retirement account, you'll build the balance without a second thought. You'll never forget to make a contribution. You'll never miss the "missing" money because you've never gotten used to having it. Once you know how much money you want to contribute to your retirement accounts, "set it and forget it," at least in the short-term.

Payroll Deductions

The easiest way to automate retirement savings is through payroll deductions. If your employer offers a retirement plan, the setup is simple; enroll in the plan as soon as you're eligible and establish your regular contribution.

When you don't have access to an employer-based retirement plan but your employer does offer direct deposit, you can still set up automatic contributions by splitting your paycheck. Most companies will let you split your paycheck between two different accounts (and sometimes more). In this case, you'll need to set up your own individual retirement account (or IRA; more on that coming up). Then you can redirect part of your paycheck into your IRA. Check with your employer's human resources department to see whether you have this option.

Recurring Transfers

If you're self-employed or can't make automatic contributions through an employer, you can set them up on your own. To do that, you'll need to create a retirement account for yourself: an IRA if you're an employee or one from a range of options (discussed in a moment) if you're self-employed. After you set up the retirement account, you can fund it with automatic transfers from a checking or savings account, available with online banking.

To make this even easier, you can open your retirement account with a robo-advisor such as Betterment (www.betterment.com) or Wealthfront (www.wealthfront.com). These low-cost, no minimum balance options help you get started quickly, and let you easily make changes to your account through an app.

Periodic Check-Ins

Check in on your retirement account balance periodically, at least once a year. Look at your investment returns and the impact of fees to see whether your savings are on track. Annual check-ins are also a good time to increase your automatic contributions, even if it's just by 1 percent. Many employers offer automatic contribution escalation, which lets you set an automatic annual percentage increase to boost your savings without having to think about it. When you're saving for retirement, tiny increases in your contributions can transform into tens of thousands of dollars over time.

GROW YOUR NEST EGG WITH COMPOUNDING

When you first open a retirement (or really any) savings or investment account, you're planting "money seeds." Over time, that seed money grows, branches out, and produces more seeds for you to plant. Every extra dollar you put in acts like fertilizer, increasing the opportunity for your money to grow bigger and faster. The longer those seeds stay firmly in the account, the bigger your money tree will grow.

That growth is called compounding, and it's how nest eggs get bigger over time. Compounding is the reason that every financial advisor in the world recommends to start saving as early as possible for retirement. Compounding depends on time, and more is always better here.

Plus, the compounding effect continues even after you retire. The money in your retirement accounts needs to last for decades—and that means a portion of it will keep growing on its own.

Removing Tax "Friction"

In regular (nonretirement) savings and investment accounts, taxes are the biggest barrier to earnings. Retirement accounts do away with that obstacle. Money that stays inside those accounts is not subject to current taxation at all. That lets your money compound much more quickly.

Let's compare what a big difference the tax-free growth can make. Suppose you save $1,000 per month for thirty years, and that your savings earns 6 percent returns annually (that's a conservative estimated return). In a tax-deferred retirement account, you'd end up with a balance of $1,004,515 (comprised of $360,000 from your contributions and $645,620 in compounded earnings). The ending balance in a regular taxable account would look very different. The balance after thirty years would come to only $743,051 (using 22 percent federal and 5 percent state tax rates). That's a difference of more than $260,000!

Don't Miss Out on Tax Credits

Many people don't know that there's a special tax credit for retirement savers that goes above and beyond all of the regular tax benefits. The Saver's Credit gives you a tax break equal to 50 percent, 20 percent, or 10 percent (depending on your income) of your retirement plan contributions up to $2,000. Unlike a tax deduction, that tax credit shaves money directly off your tax bill for instant extra savings.

Start *Now*

Here's the real secret to a flush retirement: time. The more time your savings have to grow, the less money you actually have to put away. In fact, if you start early and then stop after twenty years, you'll have more money than someone who saves more but starts twenty years later. That's why the answer to the question "When should I start saving for retirement?" will always be *right now*.

Look at the difference time can make: If you save just $200 a month for forty years, and your money earns 6 percent returns annually, you'll have around $394,000. But if you start twenty years later (giving you just twenty years of compounding) and save $800 per month—four times as much per month—you'll earn only around $374,000. In the first scenario, you contribute $96,000 less but end up with $20,000 more. That's the power of time.

MAKE CATCH-UP CONTRIBUTIONS

Whether you feel like your retirement savings are falling behind or you just want to stash as much money as possible in tax-advantaged accounts, as soon as you turn fifty you'll have the opportunity to put away some extra money. The IRS lets the fifty-plus crowd make catch-up contributions to most types of retirement accounts over and above the regular limits.

The biggest catch-up contributions are available for people with employer-based retirement plans, including 401(k), 403(b), and 457(b) plans. During the year that you turn fifty, you can contribute up to an extra $6,000 (the 2019 limit) to your account as long as your employer allows it (and around 97 percent of employers do). Be aware that even employers who offer matching contributions usually do not apply the match to catch-up contributions. You can check with your plan administrator to find out whether and how your plan handles catch-up contributions.

If you work for a small employer who offers a SIMPLE retirement plan, the catch-up contribution is limited to $3,000 extra for employees aged fifty and older, as long as the employer allows it.

Catch-up contributions are also available for IRAs (individual retirement accounts) and HSAs (health savings accounts). Whether you have a traditional or a Roth IRA, you can contribute an extra $1,000 (as of 2019) every year as a catch-up contribution once you reach age fifty. If you're eligible to contribute to both an employer plan (like a 401(k) plan) and an IRA, you may be able to make catch-up contributions to both (there are a lot of rules surrounding this double dip, so check with your tax accountant). As for HSAs, during the year you turn fifty-five, you can start making extra catch-up contributions of $1,000 every year.

NONRETIREMENT ACCOUNTS COUNT TOO

While there's a limit to how much you can stash in tax-advantaged retirement accounts, you can save as much as you want to in regular investment and savings accounts. Though these accounts won't qualify for special tax treatment, they'll still benefit from compounding. Just like with your retirement accounts, the sooner you start building up regular savings and investments, the better they'll fare.

Investing Is Not Saving

People use the terms "investing" and "saving" interchangeably, but the two are not the same. Investing means buying assets that you hope will grow in value, but that run the risk of losing value or even becoming worthless. Saving means putting money aside for later, somewhere that it can't be lost, like an FDIC insured bank account.

Don't Neglect Emergency Savings

Before you start investing outside of your retirement accounts, build up a substantial emergency savings fund. The general rule of thumb is to save three to six months of living expenses (rent or mortgage, utilities, food, medicine, etc.) in an emergency fund. This is the money you'll need if you suddenly lose your job or can't work temporarily due to a health issue, for example. You can also use this fund to cover a large, unexpected expense (such as a blown hot water heater or your dog's hip surgery) so you can avoid increasing credit card debt. Though it might be tempting, avoid tapping into this money for anything that doesn't qualify as an emergency.

If you're the sole earner in the household, it makes sense to save more; in two-earner households, you can get away with slightly smaller emergency funds. If you do eventually use some or all of your emergency fund, replenish it as soon as you can.

Micro-Investing Can Get You Going

Micro-investing involves tiny bits of money that add up over time. Many of these easy-to-use apps have you connect a debit or credit card, and then they "round up" your transactions (like turning a $3.75 purchase into $4.00) and automatically transfer the difference (following that example, 25 cents) into an investment account. You can also set up micro transfers from your bank account. Micro-investing apps include Acorns, Robinhood, and Stash.

Big Picture Diversification

Once you've got your retirement savings maxed out, emergency savings built up, and debt under control, it's time to start investing. Thanks to low-cost exchange-traded funds and mutual funds, you can get started with very little money. The trick is to make sure that your outside-retirement investing strategy complements (rather than copies) your inside-retirement investing strategy.

Before you start investing, take a look at the kinds of assets you already hold. If your retirement savings are invested 100 percent in stocks or in a mix of 80 percent stocks/20 percent bonds, it makes sense to start investing in a different asset class (like real estate) for more diversification.

EMPLOYER-SPONSORED RETIREMENT PLANS

Use Your Benefits

According to the US Bureau of Labor Statistics,

- 51 percent of private employers offer defined contribution retirement plans to their employees.
- 4 percent offer defined benefit plans.
- 13 percent offer both.

Larger companies (with one hundred or more employees) are more likely to offer retirement plans. Full-time employees have more access to these plans than part-time employees.

If you have access to a retirement plan through your employer and are not taking advantage of it, enroll as soon as you possibly can, especially if the employer offers matching contributions.

PENSIONS

Though pensions are becoming increasingly rare, they still cover millions of people, including many government employees. Pensions, also known as defined benefit plans, promise specific guaranteed payments to eligible employees when they retire. Employers retain full control over the plan. They make all of the contributions, decide where and how the plan funds will be invested, and set the formula to determine future benefits. It's the employer's responsibility to make every guaranteed pension payment for all retired employees.

Vesting

Pensions are normally offered to long-term employees. To receive the full pension payouts, employees have to be fully vested. Vesting means that rights to the pension account transfer to the employee from the employer, and this usually only happens after the employee has worked for the company for many years. Some companies use a gradual (or staged) vesting schedule, allowing employees to earn bigger pieces of the pension every year they work there until they are fully vested. For example, pension benefits could start vesting on the employee's ten-year anniversary and increase to 100 percent over the following ten years.

Periodic Payout or Lump Sum

Some employers offer you the option of choosing whether you want ongoing annuity payments or a one-time lump sum from your pension. Choosing which type of payment to take is a major decision. The binding choice you make now (you cannot change your mind) will affect your future financial security.

It's tempting to go with the lump sum, especially if you think you can avoid spending it and invest it well enough to generate more cash flow than you'd get from the annuity. Taking the lump sum comes with some serious drawbacks—especially if you don't immediately roll it over into an IRA. For one thing, the money can feel like a windfall, and it's very common to use it up too quickly. Also, investments may not perform as well as expected or there could be a major market downturn, leaving you without enough money to live on.

With the annuity option, you'll receive guaranteed income for life, and you don't have to worry about market crashes or investment performance. This option also comes with some drawbacks, though. First, those annuity payouts depend on your employer's future financial health; if they suffer setbacks, your payments could be reduced (even if they're covered by the Pension Benefit Guaranty Corporation, the PBGC). Second, most pension annuities don't come with cost of living increases, so your fixed payments will lose purchase power due to inflation. Even with these potential drawbacks, though, it's almost always better to stick with the annuity payments than to take the lump sum—especially if your life expectancy is long.

Defined Contribution versus Defined Benefit

With a defined contribution plan, you know how much you're putting into the plan, but not what you'll eventually get out of it. Defined benefit plans work the opposite way: You know ahead of time exactly how much your monthly payouts will be, but not how much the required contribution (usually made by the employer) will be each year.

401(K) PLANS

Many employers sponsor 401(k) plans to allow employees to funnel part of their salaries into retirement accounts and get an instant tax break. The money that goes into the 401(k) account is "pre-tax." That leads to less income taxes withheld from every paycheck. So, for example, if you earn $2,000 a week and put $100 of that into your 401(k), you'll only be taxed on $1,900. Once the money is in the

401(k) account, it grows without any tax effect. Every dollar you earn in interest, dividends, and capital gains stay in a safe, no-tax bubble until you take the money out in retirement.

Plus, because the 401(k) contributions automatically come straight out of your paycheck, you won't forget to make them. This lets you consistently fund your retirement account without a thought.

These plans are not without some drawbacks. Most 401(k) plans are burdened with high fees that eat into your savings and growth. They also come with limited investment options, usually a handful of mutual funds that may or may not fit into your overall financial plan.

Code Name: 401(k)

Ever wonder where the name 401(k) comes from? It's named after the subsection of tax code—Subsection 401(k)—written in 1978. That section was originally designed to let employees postpone paying income taxes on deferred compensation. Soon, that idea was transformed into employee retirement savings and the 401(k) plans we know today.

Take the Free Money

Many employers have matching plans for employees who participate in the 401(k) plan. When you contribute money, so do they, and those matching funds are based on how much money you put in. Sometimes the match is dollar-for-dollar, sometimes less (like 50 cents for every dollar), up to a set percentage of your salary.

For example, say your employer matches 50 cents for every dollar you contribute to the 401(k) plan, up to 6 percent of your salary. If you make $50,000 a year, the maximum match would be $3,000 (6 percent × $50,000). You would have to contribute $6,000 (over the whole year) to get the full $3,000 match. If you contributed $4,000 (over the year), they would contribute $2,000—and you would be missing out on $1,000.

So, if you don't contribute to the company 401(k) plan up to the maximum match, you are walking away from free money and the chance to supercharge your retirement savings. To make sure you take full advantage of your employer's 401(k) match, find out the rules (ask your human resources department if you're unsure). Then, contribute as much as you can to get the biggest possible match.

If you can't afford to contribute enough to get the full match right off the bat, start with what you can save. Then every three to six months, increase your contribution by 1 percent of your salary until you're eligible for the maximum match. Remember, every dollar you contribute reduces your taxable income and the amount of taxes that get taken out of your paycheck. The tax reduction helps offset the contribution, so you won't feel as big a pinch.

Don't Take Money Out Early

Technically, you're allowed to withdraw or borrow money from your 401(k) under certain conditions. Financially, it's a big—and very common—mistake. Even if you do pay yourself back in full, with interest, your nest egg will suffer.

If you simply withdraw the money before age fifty-nine-and-a-half, you'll be hit with a 10 percent penalty (some hardship exceptions apply) plus federal and state income taxes; that means you'll lose around 30 percent of your withdrawal to the IRS. On top of that, your nest egg will lose momentum that it can never get back; you'll miss out on years (maybe decades) of compounding.

Loans come with their own set of problems. For one thing, you have to start paying a 401(k) loan back with your next paycheck. You'll also have to pay interest on the loan, which is interest paid to yourself, but that's much less than your money would have been earning if you hadn't taken it out. Some employer plans will not let you continue savings while the loan is outstanding, so you'll lose all that savings time. And if you leave that job for any reason, you have to pay the loan back in full or be hit with the 10 percent penalty and income taxes.

What to Do When You Change Jobs

If you leave your job for any reason, you can take your 401(k) with you or leave it in the old plan. Pick that first option and take it with you. Now that people change jobs more frequently than during the heyday of the company pension, it's normal to have a bunch of old 401(k) accounts lying around with former employers. Doing nothing with old 401(k) funds can wind up costing your retirement savings in several ways:

- You're paying more fees.
- You may be double-invested in the same funds, reducing your diversification and putting your nest egg at greater risk.
- You may find it harder to track overall progress and make appropriate adjustments.
- You have less control over your money.

When you leave a job, take your 401(k) with you right away and put it into a rollover IRA or (if allowed) into your new 401(k) plan. The rules for rollovers are strict, so make sure you follow them carefully to avoid any tax penalties.

A Quick Word about Roth 401(k) Plans

Some employers offer 401(k) plans with a slight twist known as "Roth." With a Roth 401(k) plan, you can still have regular contributions taken out of your paycheck. You still choose from a menu of investment options. The twist comes into play with tax treatment.

Unlike regular 401(k) plans, Roth 401(k) plans don't reduce your tax bill now. Your contributions don't lower your taxable income *now*. That difference comes with a big future payoff. Money you take out of your Roth 401(k) in retirement is totally tax-free. You will not be taxed on any of the earnings or any withdrawals. You will, however, be required to take RMDs (required minimum distributions), just like with a regular 401(k) plan. To avoid that, you can roll over your Roth 401(k) into a Roth IRA before the RMDs kick in.

403(B) AND 457 PLANS

People who work in the public sector (such as in public schools, non-profits, or governments) have access to slightly different employer-based retirement plans. There are two main plans: 403(b) plans and 457 plans. The two work similarly but come with some striking differences. Plus, if your employer offers both, you can contribute fully to both plans.

403(b) Plans

A 403(b) plan works similarly to a 401(k) plan, but with some key differences. These plans, also known as tax-sheltered annuities (TSAs), give public employees the opportunity to save for retirement.

Like 401(k) plans, employees can make pre-tax contributions directly out of their salaries (limited by current IRS guidelines), and their employers may offer matching contributions (this is less common with 403(b) plans). The employees can choose the risk-level (such as aggressive, conservative, or balanced) for their retirement investment portfolios.

Then there are the differences. With a 403(b) plan, employees can invest in mutual funds or *annuities*. There's also an extra catch-up contribution available for employees with more than fifteen years of service. That extra contribution, known as the maximum allowable contribution (MAC), lets long-term employees contribute up to $3,000 extra per year for a total MAC of $15,000. The MAC is over and above any age-related catch-up contributions.

457 Plans

Offered by governments and some nonprofits, 457 plans also work similarly to 401(k) plans. Employees make contributions with pre-tax dollars, and their money grows tax-deferred. But because these are "nonqualified" plans, specific issues such as catch-up contributions and early withdrawals are handled differently. For example, if you pull money out before age fifty-nine-and-a-half, you won't get hit with a 10 percent tax penalty (though you will still have to pay regular income taxes on the withdrawal).

Catch-up contributions work differently too. Employers have the *option* of allowing you to make regular catch-up contributions when you reach age fifty. There's also a special extra catch-up provision that employers can offer called the "last three-year catch-up." With that, you can contribute twice the regular contribution limit during the last three years before the plan's retirement age.

INDIVIDUAL RETIREMENT ACCOUNTS (IRAS)

You're on Your Own

If you like having total control over your retirement investments, an IRA (Individual Retirement Account) is the right savings vehicle for you. Anyone can set up and fund an IRA as long as she or he has earned income. These special tax-advantaged accounts have been available since 1975, but they've gotten much more popular over the past twenty years or so because they're so flexible and easy to set up. The one drawback: Annual contributions are pretty paltry compared to other retirement account options. But if you don't have access to an employer-based plan, an IRA gives your money a place to grow without being interrupted by taxes.

TRADITIONAL IRA

Traditional (or regular) IRAs give most people (depending on your earnings) a current tax break plus tax-deferred earnings (for everyone) inside the account. Instead of paying taxes on earnings every year, like in regular investment accounts, your money compounds without any tax drag. That allows your nest egg to grow bigger, faster.

If you can't make a tax-deductible IRA contribution, you have the option of making a nondeductible contribution. Those contributions won't be taxed when you withdraw them (but the account earnings still will be) as long as you fill out IRS Form 8606 to give them a record of your after-tax contributions. You don't want to pay extra taxes once you start taking money out.

How Withdrawals Are Taxed

Once you're at least age fifty-nine-and-a-half, you can start taking withdrawals from your IRA. In most cases, every dollar you withdraw will count as taxable income and be subject to regular income taxes based on your tax rate at the time. Most providers will let you have income taxes withheld on your withdrawals, similar to how you had them withheld from your paycheck.

If you take withdrawals before age fifty-nine-and-a-half, you'll have to pay taxes on that money plus a 10 percent IRS penalty unless a special situation applies. Then, you'll still be on the hook for regular income taxes, but you won't be hit with the 10 percent penalty.

Special situations that qualify for penalty-free withdrawal of funds from your IRA include the following:

- Qualified higher education expenses
- First-time home purchases (up to $10,000)
- Health insurance premiums paid during a period of unemployment
- Divorce, with a properly executed qualified domestic relations order (QDRO)

To make sure you can make an early withdrawal without incurring penalties, consult your tax professional.

Take Your RMDs

Once you turn seventy-and-a-half, you must start taking money out of your IRA or face stiff tax penalties. Those RMDs (required minimum distributions) are calculated based on your age and the balance of your IRA accounts.

If you and your spouse are both required to take RMDs, you have to figure them out separately and take the money out of your individual accounts. Many people mistakenly believe that they can pull money to cover all the RMDs out of one spouse's account. Doing that results in tax penalties for the other spouse, who is considered to have taken no RMD.

Can You Have an IRA If You Have a 401(k)?

You can contribute to an IRA even if you have access to a 401(k) plan through your employer. However, depending on your income level, you might not be able to make tax-deductible contributions to a traditional IRA or any contributions to a Roth IRA. The limits change frequently, so check with your tax advisor or visit the IRS website for the latest details.

ROTH IRA

You won't get a current tax break on contributions to a Roth IRA, but you will get tax-*free* income in retirement. That "free" part includes both your contributions and 100 percent of the growth and earnings, as long as you play by the withdrawal rules.

In addition to the tax-free income advantage, Roth IRA withdrawals won't increase your taxable income. That can help you avoid paying taxes on Social Security benefits and higher Medicare premiums, both of which are based on taxable income.

Your Income May Limit Contributions

People with high incomes hit a roadblock when it comes to Roth IRA contributions. Once your modified adjusted gross income (MAGI), which is basically your taxable income with a bunch of deductions added back in, reaches a preset limit, the amount you can contribute to a Roth starts to phase out. When your MAGI hits the upper limit, you can't contribute anything to a Roth IRA. Those limit change every year, and they depend on your tax filing status (such as married filing jointly, head of household, or single).

There is a workaround, known as a "backdoor Roth," which lets you skirt the rule and fund a Roth IRA. To use this legal loophole, you make a contribution to a traditional IRA, then roll over that contribution to a Roth IRA. If your traditional IRA contributions were tax deductible or produced earnings, you may have to pay income taxes on the conversion. Though this workaround seems simple, the rules can get a little tricky, so it's best to consult a tax specialist before using the backdoor Roth strategy.

Tax-Free, Optional Withdrawals

Because you've already paid taxes on the money you put into the Roth IRA, you can take that money out at any time without taking a tax hit. That applies to your contributions only, though. If you take out earnings before age fifty-nine-and-a-half, you will have to pay taxes and possibly tax penalties.

To score totally tax-free earnings, the Roth IRA account must have been open for at least five years *and* you have to be at least fifty-nine-and-a-half years old when you make the withdrawal.

If you're not old enough but have had the Roth IRA for at least five years, there are some situations where you can still completely sidestep taxes, such as withdrawing up to $10,000 for a first-time home purchase. You can find the complete rules on the IRS website (www.irs.gov).

Plus, unlike other retirement accounts, Roth IRAs are not subject to RMDs; you can leave the money in the account for as long as you want, and never have to make withdrawals that you don't want to make.

HOW TO OPEN AN IRA

It takes about ten minutes to open an IRA online, and only a little longer in person. IRAs are available at virtually all banks, credit unions, and brokerage firms, so you'll have a lot of options to choose from. Before you get started, though, you'll have to make some important decisions, such as whether you want to open a traditional IRA or a Roth IRA and where you want to park your IRA. Once you have your account set up, you can start funding it and investing those funds right away.

Traditional IRA or Roth IRA?

Most people focus on the taxation differences when choosing between traditional and Roth accounts, but the flexibility factor can be just as important. The standard advice has you consider whether you think your tax rates are higher now or will be higher in the future. That leads most people toward the traditional IRA for the current tax benefit (even in years with relatively low tax rates). Remember, though, that paying tax on Roth contributions now gives you tax-*free* earnings in the future.

Roth IRAs also offer more flexibility when it comes to withdrawing your money. You can take out money you contributed (but not earnings on the account) at any time with no tax consequences. Plus, you never have to take withdrawals when you don't want to. If you need to access some of your money before retirement, it's easier and cheaper with a Roth IRA.

Choose the Institution

When you're looking for somewhere to stash your retirement savings, consider these important questions:

- Does the provider offer a variety of no-cost or low-cost mutual and exchange-traded funds?
- Are there monthly (or annual) account maintenance fees?
- What are the minimum investment requirements?
- Is the website easy to use?
- Do they offer plenty of free analysis tools and educational resources?
- What are the trading fees?
- How often do you plan to make trades or rebalance your portfolio?
- Do you want to use a robo-advisor?
- Do you want access to financial advisors, either by phone or in person?

Some of the best, most popular providers for more active investors include Ally Invest (www.ally.com/invest), Fidelity (www.fidelity.com), and TD Ameritrade (www.tdameritrade.com). If you prefer to go the robo-advisor route, good options include Ellevest (www.ellevest.com), Betterment (www.betterment.com), and Wealthfront (www.wealthfront.com).

Once you choose a provider, you can quickly and easily open your IRA online. You'll need some basic information handy, including your Social Security number and your employment details.

Fund It and Start Investing

As soon as your account is open, you can fund it. You can do that by transferring money directly from a bank or brokerage account, or rolling over other retirement funds, like an old 401(k) account, into it.

To transfer money from your bank or brokerage, you'll just need the institution routing number and your account number. You can also set up automatic transfers at the same time, which make it much easier to contribute consistently without going over the IRS contribution limits. To roll over another retirement account, contact that plan's administrator and fill out whatever forms they need. Some plans will make a direct rollover into your new IRA; others will send you a check that you will need to deposit into your IRA account within sixty days to avoid tax penalties.

Once the account has been funded, it's time to start investing. If you're using a robo-advisor, after answering some questions about your time frame and risk tolerance, it will choose investments for you. If you plan to make your own investment choices, the easiest way to get started is with no-cost (or low-cost) exchange-traded funds or index mutual funds.

SELF-DIRECTED IRA

Most IRAs are held in traditional brokerage accounts, giving you easy access to stocks, bonds, mutual funds, and exchange-traded funds. Some investors prefer a broader range of options, including "alternative" investments for their retirement accounts. Self-directed IRAs were created for those people, and while they come with more choices, they also come with *a lot more risk* and some extra rules.

Other than the investments themselves, these work just like any other IRA.

Some cautions: Self-directed IRAs are more complicated to manage than regular IRAs. You have to perform your own due diligence (investment homework) for every investment. Alternative investments usually lack liquidity, meaning they're harder to convert into fast cash, and that can be a tricky issue when you're trying to take your RMDs. These accounts also usually require much larger minimum investments. There are also fewer safeguards, which can make these accounts treacherous for novice investors.

Expanded Investment Options

When you're talking about the investment choices for self-directed IRAs, it's easier to list the things you're *not allowed* to invest in: life insurance, S corporations (specially taxed corporations with fewer than 100 shareholders), and collectibles. Everything else is fair game. As long as you can find a custodian who accepts it, your self-directed IRA can invest in:

- Real estate, including rental properties
- Limited partnership shares
- Active farms and livestock (including racehorses)
- Privately held corporations
- Hedge funds
- Online lending platforms (such as www.lendingclub.com)
- Cryptocurrency (such as Bitcoin)

Basically, you can invest in anything you want except for the specifically prohibited investments.

Use Caution When Choosing a Custodian and Investments

It's harder to find a custodian for a self-directed IRA than for the standard version, and there will be more—and often much higher—fees. Those fees will vary widely depending on both the custodian and the type of investment, so do your homework to avoid costly surprises. Most providers specialize in self-directed IRAs, and often sub-specialize in a type of asset. Most big-name providers (like Vanguard and Fidelity) don't offer this service, but Charles Schwab (www.schwab.com) does, though the investment options are somewhat limited. You can start your search by looking at the IRS Approved Nonbank Trustees and Custodians list (available at www.irs.gov).

Another huge caution: Con artists specifically target self-directed IRA owners with enticing investments that seem real but are really scams. To avoid being sucked in and potentially losing your entire retirement nest egg, consider working with a trusted financial advisor experienced in the type of investment you want to buy.

Never Cross the Self-Dealing Line

When you have a self-directed IRA, you have to be especially aware of prohibited transactions. Cross one of these lines and not only will all of the tax benefits disappear, you may also be subjected to substantial IRS penalties and interest.

The number one rule with these IRAs is no self-dealing. That means you absolutely cannot under any circumstances borrow money from the account, sell assets to the account, buy assets from the account, or interact with the assets in any way. For example, say you buy a residential rental property inside your self-directed IRA. One day, you drive by and realize that the flowerbed is covered in weeds, so you stop and pull them out. You just "furnished services" to your IRA asset, a prohibited transaction. If, instead, you pay a gardener out of your personal account to do the weeding, it's still a prohibited transaction.

Other examples of prohibited transactions when you have a self-directed IRA include:

- Renting real estate to your parent or child
- Using the IRA assets as collateral for a loan
- Buying personal property (like a boat) and using it now or at any time in the future
- Buying goods or services from a company that you or your family members own

The IRS pays attention to self-directed IRAs because they're big potential moneymakers for the agency. If they find that you've put even a toe across the self-dealing line, they may consider your IRA to be "fully distributed" in the year the transaction took place, meaning the *entire* IRA no longer exists—not just the related asset. You'll have to pay current income taxes on the entire distribution (unless it's a Roth IRA) plus a 10 percent penalty if you're not yet age fifty-nine-and-a-half.

SELF-EMPLOYED OPTIONS

Boss with Benefits

If you are self-employed or own your own business, you have even more choices when it comes to retirement savings. The most beneficial plan for you depends on a number of key factors, such as whether or not you have employees, your company's annual earnings, plan administration costs, and your current age.

SEP-IRA

For self-employed people with no employees, a Simplified Employee Pension—Individual Retirement Account or SEP-IRA is the quickest, easiest, most flexible retirement plan to set up. Creating a SEP-IRA requires minimal paperwork—it's just a one-page form. There are no ongoing administrative reporting requirements for the IRS.

Best of all, these plans allow you to sock away more cash than IRAs, so your retirement savings can grow much faster. Every year, you can contribute up to 25 percent of your net self-employment earnings (there's a special calculation for this that we'll talk about in a minute) or a preset limit (which was $56,000 for 2019).

Flexibility

Flexibility may be the best feature of the SEP. That starts with timing: Once you decide you want to create a SEP, you can open and fund it at any time until your income tax return due date, including any extensions.

SEPs are also flexible when it comes to contributions. You can change the amount you contribute every year based on what's going on with your finances. If you're having a lean year, you can skip the contribution; if you're having a prosperous year, you can max it out.

Side Gigs Count Too

If you have a side gig where you're not considered an employee (meaning you don't get a paycheck with taxes taken out), the IRS counts that as a separate business. That means you are eligible to open and fund a self-employed retirement account.

The Contribution Calculation

Small business owners need to do a little math to come up with their maximum allowable SEP-IRA contributions. For this equation, you need to know three numbers:

1. Your net business income before the contribution, which must match what you reported on your income tax return (usually on Schedule C).
2. The tax deduction for one-half of your self-employment tax (you can find this on your tax return as well).
3. The reduced plan contribution rate (which accounts for the impact of the contribution on net income), which you can find in Publication 560 on the IRS website at www.irs.gov.

The IRS provides a simple worksheet for figuring out your contribution. Also, most tax software can automatically calculate your maximum contribution.

Four Easy Steps to Set Up Your SEP-IRA

The *S* in SEP-IRA stands for "simplified" for a reason: These plans are super easy to start. All it takes are four very simple steps.

1. Create your plan using IRS Form 5305-SEP, which you can download from the IRS website at www.irs.gov.
2. Open a SEP-IRA account through your bank, brokerage, or other financial institution.
3. Fund your SEP-IRA (up to the legal limit).
4. Choose your investment portfolio.

A lot of people forget to take that final step, leaving their funds in a low-interest holding account. That can put a significant dent in the plan's compounding power, so make sure to invest this money right away.

Eligible Employees

There are three criteria employees must meet to qualify as eligible for a SEP-IRA: They must be at least twenty-one, have worked for you for at least three of the past five years, and received at least the minimum annual compensation ($600 for 2019) during the current year. You can make the requirements less restrictive (for example, allowing twenty-year-olds to participate), but not more restrictive.

If You Have Employees

You can establish a SEP-IRA if you have employees, but this type of plan works best with minimal employees (no more than five). While you don't have to make contributions every year, when you do make them, you have to make them for everyone at the same rate (usually a percentage of salary); if you want to contribute 10 percent of your earnings, you have to contribute 10 percent of each participant's salary.

In these plans, *only* employers make the contributions. To do that, a separate SEP-IRA account must be set up for each eligible employee (unless they choose to cancel it). As soon as an employee becomes eligible, you have to fully inform them about the plan, disclosing all plan details. Also, unlike some other types of retirement plans, as soon as you make the contribution to an employee account, the money is 100 percent theirs; contributions vest immediately and fully.

SIMPLE IRA PLANS

SIMPLE IRA plans don't live up to their acronym (SIMPLE stands for "Savings Incentive Match PLan for Employees"—awkward, right?). While they are less complicated and a lot less expensive than 401(k) plans for small businesses, SIMPLE IRA plans come with some strict rules, lower contribution limits than SEPs and 401(k)s, and limited flexibility for employers. These can make good starter plans, and work best for small to midsize businesses that don't have too many employees (the IRS limit for SIMPLE IRA plans is 100 employees).

Two-Sided Contributions

With a SIMPLE plan, both employers and eligible employees can make contributions. Any employee who earned at least $5,000 during *any* two prior calendar years and who's expected to earn at least $5,000 in the current year is eligible (even if their employment is sporadic). Participation is mandatory for eligible employees; contributions are optional. Employee contributions are made through payroll deductions, managed by the employer.

Employers can choose between doing either of the following:

- Mandatory fixed contributions of 2 percent of compensation (up to the annual limit) for all eligible employees.
- Making optional dollar-for-dollar matching contributions of up to 3 percent of employee compensation for any employee who contributes.

Whichever you choose, employer contributions are *required* every year, regardless of profits and cash flow. If you do the fixed 2 percent contributions, you have to make them for all employees who were eligible during the year even if they no longer work for you when you make the contributions.

How to Set Up a SIMPLE IRA Plan

SIMPLE plans have to be set up by October 1 of the year you want to start making contributions. To get started, you have to choose a plan provider, such as Fidelity (www.fidelity .com), Charles Schwab (www.schwab.com), and Vanguard (www .vanguard.com). The next step is filling out one of two IRS forms (available through your provider or at www.irs.gov) to establish your plan:

- Use Form 5305-SIMPLE if you want to designate the financial institution for contributions.
- Use Form 5304-SIMPLE if you plan to let employees decide where they want their funds (this is much less common).

The form sets out basic plan information, including eligibility rules, the ways to make contributions for employees, and the plan effective date. It also includes a model employee notification form to help you make all of the necessary disclosures to your employees and get their contribution amounts.

The plan provider will help you with all of the paperwork and help you set up individual SIMPLE IRA accounts for each employee. Once the plan and accounts are created, contact your payroll company to start making automatic salary deferrals for every employee who wants to make contributions. The payroll company can also help you make the required employer contributions.

SOLO 401(K) PLANS

Like the name spells out, solo 401(k) plans are for self-employed people with no employees; you *cannot* use this plan if you have any employees, unless that employee is your spouse. These plans are perfect for consultants and contractors who want to sock away a lot of money for retirement. They're fairly simple to set up and have ongoing minimal reporting requirements.

You're the Employee and the Employer

When you have a solo 401(k), you get to make two rounds of contributions: once as the employer, and once as the employee. The employee contribution limits are the same as for any other 401(k) plan ($19,000 with a catch-up contribution of $6,000 for 2019). Keep in mind that the contribution limits to 401(k) plans are linked to the person, not the plan. If your solo 401(k) is for a side gig and you also participate in a 401(k) plan at work, the employee contribution limit covers the two combined. For example, if the limit were $19,000, and you contributed $15,000 to your outside employer's plan, you could only contribute $4,000 on the employee side of your solo 401(k).

On the employer side, you can make another contribution based on profit-sharing. That contribution can be up to 25 percent of your net self-employment income (which calls for a little math) or your compensation (if you pay yourself a regular paycheck). Net self-employment income here means the net profit from your business minus half of your self-employment taxes minus the plan contributions you made. This second dip allows you to stash a lot more money in your retirement account every year (up to $56,000 plus the $6,000 catch-up for 2019).

Seven Steps to Set Up Your Solo 401(k)

You can open and start funding your solo 401(k) in seven easy steps:

1. Have your Employer Identification Number (EIN) handy. If you don't have one, you can get one immediately by applying online at the IRS website (www.irs.gov).
2. Choose a plan provider, such as an online broker. Some of the best providers include Fidelity (www.fidelity.com), Charles Schwab (www.schwab.com), and Vanguard (www.vanguard.com).
3. Fill out the paperwork, including the plan adoption agreement, which is supplied by your provider. These documents can be tricky, and most providers will walk you through this step.
4. Create the required employee disclosures. You can find the information the disclosures need to include on the IRS website at www.irs.gov or through your plan provider.

5. Open the solo 401(k) account. It's best to do this by December 31 of the year you want to start the plan, though technically you can do this by the tax-filing deadline (for example, April 15, 2020 for a 2019 plan).
6. Make contributions to the plan. Employee contributions must be made by December 31; employer contributions can be made by the tax-filing deadline.
7. Choose investments. Don't forget this important step and leave your money uninvested.

DEFINED BENEFIT PLANS

Defined benefit plans are rare among self-employed individuals, but they can be remarkable retirement savings tools in specific situations. If you have a lot of income and no employees, these plans give you the most flexibility and allow the largest tax-deductible contributions (by far), especially beneficial if you're closing in on retirement. Administrative costs may be steep because you have to hire an actuary to figure out the numbers every year. The biggest plus: These pensions offer guaranteed cash flow streams in retirement.

Generous Benefit Limits

Defined benefit plans promise a specific payout during retirement. To fund the plan properly, contributions are based on a whole host of factors, including:

- Compensation
- Current age
- Expected retirement age

- Expected returns on the plan investments
- Planned benefit payouts

Because these plans are benefit based, benefit limits apply rather than annual contribution limits. Those benefit limits can be very generous: The IRS defines them as the lesser of your average compensation for your three highest consecutive annual earnings or $225,000 (as of 2019). That means you can fund your retirement account based on future *guaranteed* pension payouts of up to $225,000 per year (based on current IRS guidelines), and the limit gets a cost-of-living adjustment annually.

To get those future benefits, current contributions can be as big as they need to be. This allows high-earning self-employed individuals to stash insane amounts of money ($100,000 per year, for example) away for retirement.

Managing a Defined Benefit Plan

Defined benefit plans are much more complicated than other types of retirement plans. There's more paperwork, and they cost quite a bit to set up and maintain. It can also take quite a while to get the set-up documents in order, so get started at least three months before you want to create your plan.

The plan has to be set up by December 31 of the year you want to start making contributions, but the contributions can be delayed until the due date of the business tax return. Fewer providers offer defined benefit plans than other types of retirement plans, but those that do really know all the ins and outs. Defined benefit plan providers include Charles Schwab (www .schwab.com) and Dedicated Defined Benefit Services (www .dedicated-db.com).

Every year, you'll have to file IRS Form 5500, with the help of an experienced financial professional. Typically, plan providers will handle the paperwork for you and charge you a hefty fee.

Defined benefit plans can only be canceled early for "valid business reasons," which may include retiring earlier than expected and closing down your business. Consult a tax attorney before terminating your plan, as the IRS imposes penalties for "invalid" terminations and may disallow all of the prior tax deductions.

HEALTH SAVINGS ACCOUNTS (HSAS)

The Secret Retirement Stash

Virtually everyone will need to pay for medical care at some point, and those costs can be outrageously high. Funding an HSA as part of your overall retirement planning means that you won't have to pull money out of your living expenses funds to pay for your healthcare. Plus, these accounts enjoy some pretty sweet tax advantages, making them even more beneficial for your financial picture.

TRIPLE TAX ADVANTAGES

HSAs offer a trio of solid tax benefits that boost your finances now and later, making this account a valuable addition to any retirement plan.

1. Contributions reduce your tax bill now.
2. Growth is tax-free.
3. Withdrawals are tax-free (as long as you follow the rules).

No other type of tax-advantaged account offers all three of these benefits in one.

Pre-Tax Contributions

If your employer offers an HSA plan, take advantage of it. When you make contributions this way, you're funding the account with *pre-tax* dollars. That means your contribution does not count toward taxable income, and you don't pay tax on it; your withholding taxes are reduced.

This treatment is especially beneficial for people who don't itemize medical expenses on their tax returns (and most people don't).

You get the same benefit if you DIY your HSA by opening and funding an account on your own. Contributions are tax-deductible, reducing your current taxable income and your tax bill.

Tax-Free Earnings

Most HSA accounts offer a menu of investment options, similar to 401(k) and other retirement plans. That means the money you have sitting in your HSA can earn even more money. Any money you earn inside the HSA is tax-exempt, meaning you don't have to pay any income taxes on them like you would for regular interest or dividends. Your HSA earnings build up *tax-free*, which increases the power of compounding, letting your money grow even faster.

Tax-Free Withdrawals

As long as you use the money in your HSA to pay for qualified medical expenses, your withdrawals will be 100 percent tax-free. But if you use the money for anything else, you could face tax penalties of up to 20 percent plus regular income taxes on the withdrawal amount.

And there's a beneficial twist. Once you turn sixty-five, you can use this money for anything without facing any taxes or penalties.

KNOW THE RULES

Like most tax-advantaged savings plans, HSAs come with a lot of rules. If you don't follow them to the letter, you could get hit with fines, penalties, and a bigger tax bill. Luckily (unlike many IRS rules), the guidelines for HSAs are straightforward and easy to understand.

Since the rules are subject to change, check in with the IRS website (www.irs.gov) for the most current guidelines.

Don't Confuse HSAs with FSAs

Though the initials are similar and they're both used for medical expenses, there are huge differences between HSAs and flexible spending accounts (FSAs). The biggest of those differences: the use-it or lose-it rule. Any money left in an FSA at year-end disappears. So, if you have money in an FSA, spend every penny.

The HDHP Rule

HSAs can only be used in connection with high-deductible health plans (HDHPs). The IRS has a specific definition for what counts as an HDHP, so make sure your plan qualifies before you open an HSA. Be aware that to be HSA-eligible, you can't be covered under any other health plan, and you can't be claimed as a dependent on someone else's tax return.

The first test involves the deductible, which is the amount you have to pay in healthcare costs before your insurance starts picking up the tab. The minimum deductible for 2019 is $1,350 for single coverage or $2,700 for family coverage.

The second test looks at the maximum annual deductible and other out-of-pocket expenses (often this includes only in-network providers). The maximums for 2019 are $6,750 for single coverage and is $13,500 for family coverage.

These dollar amounts change every year, so make sure you have the latest information. You can get more information on this in IRS Publication 969, available at their website, www.irs.gov.

Beware Family Plans That Don't Count

Some family plans have deductibles for the whole family and for each family member, where when one family member hits their individual deductible it counts for the whole family. If that is less than the IRS HDHP family coverage deductible, the plan does not qualify. That means you're not eligible to fund an HSA.

Contribution Limits

You can contribute to your HSA every year up to that year's limits. For example, in 2019 the limits were $3,500 for individuals and $7,000 for families. If you're over fifty-five (and not yet enrolled in Medicare), you can make a catch-up contribution of $1,000. Once you're enrolled in Medicare, you can't contribute anymore.

Employer Contributions Count Toward the Limit

If you're lucky enough to have an employer who contributes to your HSA, deduct that contribution from your annual limit. For example, if your HSA contribution limit is $3,500 and your employer contributes $500, you can't contribute more than $3,000.

If you make excess contributions, meaning you put more money in than the limit allows, you have to pay regular income taxes on the amount *plus* a penalty tax (6 percent as of 2019) every year until you fix the problem. If you notice the problem before the tax filing deadline for the year, withdraw the excess contribution and any related earnings, and report the earnings as income on your tax return. The fix is more complicated when the excess contribution was made in a prior tax year, so it's best to consult a tax professional for help.

Medical Spending

In order to avoid taxes and tax penalties, use HSA money only for eligible medical expenses. Using the money for anything else (before age sixty-five) triggers a tax bill or a request for you to pay back the HSA.

Luckily, that list of eligible expenses includes most things you'd expect, and a couple of nice surprises. Here are just some of the things you can use your HSA money for:

- Prescription drugs
- Premiums for long-term care insurance
- Copays for doctor visits
- Acupuncture
- Chiropractor
- Bandages
- Eyeglasses and contact lenses (and saline solution)
- Pregnancy tests
- Breast pumps
- Mental health services
- Medical-related travel expenses (such as taking a ride service to the dentist)

You can use HSA funds to cover healthcare expenses for yourself, your spouse, and your dependents. Be aware that you can't pay medical bills dating from before you opened the HSA.

Free(ish) Money Once You Hit Age Sixty-Five

Here's one of the greatest features of HSAs: Once you're sixty-five years old, you can pull out the money for *any reason* without facing tax penalties. This can add another stress-free income source to your retirement budget.

HOW TO OPEN YOUR OWN HSA

If you're self-employed or your employer doesn't offer an HSA, you can set up one for yourself (as long as you qualify). There are many qualified custodians to choose from. The trick lies in choosing the best account for your current situation. Whichever custodian you go with, make sure you fully understand all of the fees, balance requirements, investment options, and how you can pay (or be reimbursed) for medical expenses.

Are You a Medical Spender or Saver?

To get the best account fit, you need to know whether you'll be using your HSA mainly to pay current medical bills or as a future savings vehicle. If you're using a lot of healthcare services now (common for people with children, chronic illnesses, or regular prescriptions), you're a medical spender. If you rarely spend money on healthcare, you're a medical saver. That distinction will help you get the most out of your HSA.

Spenders do best with no-fee or low-fee HSAs. They don't have to worry as much about investment options because they'll be using the money in the account to cover expenses. Still, you want to make sure the custodian offers low-cost investment options that fit into your overall portfolio for the money that you don't spend now.

Savers do best with a variety of robust investment choices. Make sure the options include no-fee or low-fee ETFs (exchange-traded funds) or mutual funds that work with your other retirement investments. Keep an eye on fees and trading costs, which can eat into your savings.

Opening the Account

Once you choose an HSA custodian, you'll have to fill out some paperwork to open your account. Most custodians let you do this online. You can also go to the bank (or credit union or brokerage) and fill out paperwork in person.

You'll need to have the following information handy:

- Your Social Security number
- Your HDHP (high-deductible health plan) provider
- Bank routing and accountant numbers
- Identification (you can usually just take a picture of your license and upload it)

Once the account is open, you need to fund it. The easiest way is to set up automatic transfers to the account, making sure you don't go over the annual contribution limit.

DESIGN YOUR RETIREMENT PORTFOLIO AT ANY AGE

Your Future Wealth Plan

The best investments for your retirement portfolio depend mainly on time. Your current age and your planned retirement age determine your time horizon, and that is the number one factor ruling the investment strategy. As your time horizon shortens, you'll start shifting gradually from aggressive growth toward income preservation, which involves reducing risk of loss but also lowers potential returns.

The two pieces you'll work with are asset allocation and diversification. Asset allocation refers to different types of assets (such as stocks, bonds, cash, and real estate) and how much room each takes up in your portfolio. For example, you could have 75 percent stocks, 10 percent bonds, 10 percent real estate, and 5 percent cash. Diversification involves choosing a variety of investments inside each asset class. Your strategy will include both asset allocation and diversification. Periodically (at least once a year), you'll check in on your portfolio to make sure your asset allocation is still in line with your strategy.

TWENTY-FIVE TO FORTY-FIVE YEARS TO GO

When you have plenty of time on your side, that's the time to go all in on aggressive investing. Your nest egg can stand temporary dips in investment values because it has decades to recover from losses and bounce back even stronger. If you can't stand the ups and downs of market volatility, don't watch. Playing it safe now might reduce the risk of loss, but it will also increase the risk that your money won't grow big or fast enough to provide you with a secure retirement.

With this much time, you can dedicate 80 percent to 95 percent of your retirement portfolio to stocks and split the rest between real estate and bonds. Then, the easiest way to diversify is by investing in index mutual funds and exchange-traded funds.

Stock Up on Stocks

Over the long term, stocks have produced higher returns than any other asset class (in the US). Having a diversified stock portfolio helps reduce the impact of market declines. That's because even during a downward spiral, some companies and industries will fare better than others. Investing in index funds and ETFs, especially those with the lowest expense ratios, is the best way to stay diversified.

At this stage, with plenty of time to spare, you could consider these fund categories:

- Aggressive growth
- Emerging markets
- Small-cap and mid-cap stocks
- Specialty funds

Before investing in any fund, do some research. Good resources include Morningstar (www.morningstar.com), Reuters (www.reuters .com, under the Markets tab), and Kiplinger (www.kiplinger.com). Your brokerage firm probably also has a set of investment screening tools and other resources you can use to research your options before you buy shares.

Use Real Estate and Bonds for an Anchor

Keeping a toe in lower risk assets could soften the blow of stock market downturns. There are hundreds of bond funds and dozens of funds that hold real estate investment trusts (REITs). Since the purpose of this portion of your portfolio is to add stability, avoid choosing riskier options such as high-yield bond funds or niche REITs. For "safe" bond funds, you can go with investment-grade corporate bonds or federal government bonds; don't bother with municipal bonds in your retirement accounts because they're tax-exempt anyway. To add in some real estate holdings, look at index REIT funds and ETFs.

TEN TO TWENTY-FIVE YEARS TO GO

Even if you got a late start, you still have some time to build up a size-able nest egg with maxed-out savings and smart investing. However, as you're moving closer to your retirement age, take a slightly more conservative approach with your portfolio. At this point, your asset allocation will begin down-shifting toward 55 percent to 80 percent stocks with the balance split between real estate and bonds. How you allocate your funds depends on a combination of your overall net worth, retirement investment performance to date, your time horizon (e.g., if retirement is closer to ten years than twenty-five, aim toward the lower stock percentage).

Stock Shifts

With at least ten years to go until you retire and a smaller percent-age devoted toward stocks, your portfolio can handle a 100 percent growth focus on the stock side. There's plenty of time to rebound from downturns while you let your nest egg continue to build value. If you tend to be risk-averse, you can start moving out of more aggressive, riskier positions without giving up growth altogether. Look at broader market funds, value funds, growth funds (without "aggressive" in the name), and dividend growth funds for less risky growth. Don't ditch aggressive growth completely, though; with this much time left, keep at least some of your stockpile invested in aggressive growth.

Build In Balance with Bonds and Real Estate

With a bigger portion of your portfolio allocated to bonds and real estate, you'll want broad diversity in your investments. On the bond side, go for a mix of investment-grade corporate bonds, US government bonds, and highly rated global (or international) bond funds. In addition to spreading out the types of bonds, make sure you also diversify maturities (how long until the bonds come due), with an emphasis on shorter-term securities. You'll also want to diversify your real estate investments with different types of residential and commercial REITs. REITs typically specialize in one type of real estate (such as office buildings, warehouses, student housing, or residential rental apartments), so a mix of REITs or REIT funds gives you broad exposure to different types of real estate.

ONE TO TEN YEARS TO GO

When retirement is right around the corner, you'll want to make a sharp turn toward wealth preservation. That doesn't mean ditching stocks altogether; after all, you still have decades ahead of you, so your nest egg still needs some growth potential. Now you'll tone down your more aggressive investments to reduce the risk of big losses, and add in safer, steadier funds. Your asset allocation model will be more bond and real estate heavy, but maintain enough growth stocks to keep building up your nest egg. Aim for 35 percent to 50 percent in stocks, reducing the percentage gradually as you near retirement, with the balance of your portfolio in bonds and REITs.

This is a good time to consult with a financial advisor (go with a fee-based fiduciary advisor), who can look at your overall financial situation (including your nonretirement assets, debt level, budgetary needs, etc.) and make recommendations for your retirement nest egg.

You can also start making catch-up contributions to your retirement accounts.

More Stable Stocks

To balance risk reduction and sustained growth, start moving out of aggressive stock investments and into more conservative stock funds that prioritize stability and income. These funds hold blue-chip stocks, meaning they hold long-established companies with strong market positions that are better able to weather downturns. You won't see explosive growth in stock price with these investments. Rather, you'll enjoy slow and steady growth along with reliable dividends that can provide income once you cross the threshold into retirement.

Focus On Income

In the bond portion of your portfolio, income is the key word. Stock up mainly with mid- and short-term US bond market index funds or ETFs. On the long-term bond side, Treasury Inflation-Protected Securities (TIPS) make a good addition to this portion of your retirement portfolio. Though the interest rates are nothing to get excited about, they do adjust periodically to keep up with inflation. Round out your bond allocation with a small investment (maybe 5 percent to 10 percent) in a high-yield corporate bond fund. Though these non-investment grade bonds pay higher interest rates, they come with higher default risk, even though many are issued by solid corporations.

REITs and REIT funds offer three distinct benefits that earn them a large slice of the portfolio:

1. Reliable income
2. Strong growth potential
3. Good inflation hedge

Keeping Up with Inflation

That last point—an inflation hedge—is especially important in a retirement nest egg. REIT income is generally based on underlying property rental income, and as general prices go up, so do rents. That means your REIT income stream has a great shot of keeping pace with (or even outpacing) inflation.

ONCE YOU RETIRE

After you've retired, your focus will change again, this time toward making your money last as long as possible. Now, you want to do everything you can to protect your nest egg from market drops and other economic threats while beefing up its income-producing power. One of the best ways to do both things is with a bucket strategy.

Using a bucket strategy keeps your investments on track for the long haul. This involves splitting your nest egg into three "buckets," each with a different financial purpose and plan.

Bucket One

This bucket will hold eighteen to thirty-six months' worth of cash to cover your living expenses over the next couple of years. This is money you can absolutely not afford to lose, so it needs to be in a 100 percent secure FDIC-insured bank account. You can put a portion of this bucket into a money market *account* (not a money market *fund*) to earn a little more interest, but not the whole amount, because withdrawals are strictly limited. This bucket is also where you'll receive (preferably through direct deposit) income from sources like Social Security, pension and annuity payments, and RMDs.

Bucket Two

This holds the money you expect to need in the next three to five years. Here, the investment focus will be on generating steady, reliable income. If you receive (and will continue to receive) sufficient guaranteed payments, this bucket won't need to hold as much money, leaving more for Bucket Three. However, if your only source of guaranteed income is Social Security, keep more money in this bucket. To walk the balance between income, growth, and safety, invest the money in this bucket conservatively with choices like investment-grade bonds and money market funds. If you're very risk-averse, include some laddered bank CDs (certificates of deposit); if you can handle a little more risk, consider including high-dividend-paying blue-chip stocks.

Bucket Three

This bucket holds your "plenty of time" money, funds you won't need to tap for at least five years. Because of the longer time horizon, this bucket concentrates on long-term stable growth. The funds in this bucket can handle more risk than the other buckets because there's time to recover from temporary setbacks. Here, investments can include primarily broad market stock funds and REITs (real estate investment trusts), preferably through index mutual funds and ETFs.

You can move money from bucket three into bucket two, or from bucket two into bucket one as you need it. If you're not sure how much money to include in each bucket or which investments to choose, a trusted fee-based fiduciary financial advisor can help you create your bucket plan.

TARGET DATE FUNDS

Target date funds were created to take some of the guesswork out of retirement investing by steadily adjusting your portfolio from riskier funds to more conservative funds as you approach retirement. These funds are named according to what your target date is, like "Target Date 2060," for example. Like regular mutual funds, these hold big baskets of different securities. Where they're different is that they focus on asset allocation as well as the underlying investments, and they periodically rebalance the portfolio to reduce risk as the target date (such as the date of your retirement) nears.

The trade-off for this hands-off portfolio is fees; target date funds can be much more expensive than index mutual funds and ETFs, and those high expenses eat into your earnings.

To or Through

There are two basic types of target date funds: "to" funds and "through" funds. A "to" fund makes its final portfolio adjustment at the target date, taking you up to retirement. After that, the fund asset allocation remains static (though individual holdings may change).

A "through" fund takes investors through retirement, so the portfolio continues adjusting well past the target date. These funds can reach their most conservative mix decades after you retire, offering opportunity for more sustained growth but also increasing risk of loss.

What You May Not Know about Target Date Funds

Here are some of the common pitfalls of target funds that most people don't realize:

- Target date funds almost always charge much higher fees than other funds.
- These funds are *not* risk-free and may suffer substantial losses, just like any other investment fund.
- Different funds with the same target date hold different investments and have different asset allocations.
- Investing in other funds along with a target date fund defeats the whole purpose of the target date fund.
- Hitting the target date *does not mean you have enough money to retire*.

AVOID THESE MAJOR MISTAKES

Don't Do This

Actions that seem harmless can completely derail your retirement savings, leaving you without enough money to retire comfortably, or even at all. The biggest misstep of all is completely ignoring the subject, which leads to substantial undersaving and the loss of years (even decades) of potential nest-egg growth. You can avoid the mistakes that have left past retirees financially insecure by facing retirement head-on with a plan.

WAITING

As soon as you start earning money, it's time to start saving for retirement. The longer you wait, the harder it will be to fund your retirement nest egg.

But it's hard to think about all that when you're just starting out and retirement seems like it's forever in the future. On top of that, retirement planning can seem confusing, filled with variables and calculations that just turn some people off.

Time is your best friend when it comes to retirement savings; procrastination is your enemy. Even if you don't have a strategy right now, and even if you're unsure about some of those variables, saving anything is better than doing nothing.

The Hurdles

Retirement seems far off and complicated. Other financial goals seem more important because they're immediate (like making rent and paying down student loans). You may feel uncomfortable with the stock market and its crazy volatility and potential to crash, wiping out the lion's share of your nest egg. It's easy to feel overwhelmed by it all, and easy to just ignore something that won't affect you for forty or fifty years.

Plus, there are so many choices to make. You have to decide whether to sign up for your employer's 401(k) plan or save on your own. Then you have to figure out how much to contribute and which investments to choose. Even if you're automatically enrolled in your employer's plan, that doesn't mean you can just forget about retirement savings. Automatic contributions are typically a very small percentage of salary (such as 1 percent or 3 percent), which won't be enough to pay for a decades-long retirement. And if you don't make investment selections, you'll wind up with the employer's default choices, and those may not be the best fit for your finances.

You Could Lose Out on More Than $425,000

When it comes to retirement savings, waiting even a few years can make a gigantic difference in the size of your nest egg. Let's look at some numbers so you can see what happens when you delay retirement savings.

Suppose you contribute $6,000 a year ($500 per month) to your retirement plan, and it earns an average 6 percent return every year until you reach age sixty-five.

If you start those savings at age twenty-five, you'll contribute $240,000 and build a nest egg of $984,286.

If you wait to start until age thirty-five, you'll put in $180,000 and finish with $502,810.

If you wait another five years and start at age forty, you'll contribute $150,000 and finish with $348,938.

Plus, even if you start late but contribute the same amount as if you'd started earlier, you'll still wind up much further behind. For example, if you start at age forty and contribute a total of $240,000 ($9,600 per year; $800 per month), your nest egg at age sixty-five will be $558,301. That's more than $425,000 *less* for retirement even though you contributed the same amount.

Don't Miss the *Free Money*

If your employer makes matching retirement contributions, you have to contribute to get that *free money*. Contribute up to the match (which is usually somewhere between 3 percent and 6 percent) to supercharge your retirement savings with *free money*. Did I mention that not contributing up to the match point means walking away from *free money*?

Take the Easy Way Out

If thinking about retirement savings gives you a headache, just do these three things today—it's easier than you think.

1. Join a plan: Either sign up for your employer's plan or open an IRA (the steps to do that are in the previous section, and it only takes about ten minutes).
2. Set up automatic transfers for 5 percent of your salary: Have your employer take the money directly out of your paycheck to make contributions or set up monthly transfers from your bank account to your IRA.
3. Pick investments: Start with a no-fee or low-fee broad stock market fund (such as an S&P 500 fund or a total market fund).

This will get you going. You will need to stay proactive moving forward by increasing your contributions and creating an investment strategy. Take advantage of any advisory services your employer offers. If you don't have access to advice through your job, talk to your accountant or connect with a financial professional to help you make a solid plan.

PULLING MONEY OUT EARLY

Loans and early withdrawals are among the biggest threats to your retirement savings. People pull money from these accounts when they feel like they're in dire financial straits. But taking money out of your retirement savings now will put you in that same desperate financial situation in the future.

The Two *Big* Consequences of Early Withdrawals

When you pull money out of retirement accounts before age fifty-nine-and-a-half, that's an early withdrawal. The first big consequence is an immediate, big tax bill. Not only does the IRS charge a 10 percent tax penalty on the vast majority of early withdrawals, you'll also have to pay federal and state income taxes on the amount you take out. Since that "income" will increase your taxable income, it could push you into a higher tax bracket, increasing your tax burden even further.

The second consequence is lost time. When you pull money out of your retirement savings, you don't just lose the withdrawal. You also lose all of its compounding power, usually decades worth of earnings. That will take a significant toll on your future financial security, reducing your eventual nest egg by tens—or even hundreds—of thousands of dollars.

The Three *Big* Risks of Borrowing from Your 401(k)

Taking out a 401(k) loan may not seem risky, but it is. Not only can the loan derail your retirement savings, it may also take a toll on your current finances. Here are the three big risks of 401(k) loans:

1. Even though you'll pay yourself back with interest, you'll still lose all of the compound earnings on the amount you pulled out; plus, that interest rate will almost certainly be lower than the returns your money could have earned.
2. Many employers don't allow you to make contributions to your 401(k) while you have an outstanding loan, so you'll lose the ability to save; plus, repayment starts immediately and comes right out of your paycheck, which many borrowers are not prepared for.
3. If you leave or lose your job for any reason, you have to pay the full loan back or the IRS will treat it like an early withdrawal and charge taxes and penalties.

If you're considering borrowing money from your retirement account, try to find any other way to get the money you need.

NOT PAYING ATTENTION TO FEES

Your retirement accounts and the investments they hold are subject to lots of fees, and those fees eat away at your investment returns. For example, if you're earning 6 percent returns but paying 2 percent in fees, your money is really only increasing by 4 percent. While 1 percent or 2 percent may not seem like a lot, it really adds up over the forty or fifty years during which your money is in the retirement account. According to NerdWallet (www.nerdwallet.com), paying as little as 1 percent in fees could cost you more than $500,000 over forty years!

Even though your investment options are more limited with employer-based plans than they are with IRAs, you can still seek out lower-cost funds. Stick with no-load (meaning no commission) mutual funds. Choose funds with lower expense ratios (or fund fees), which are normally charged as a percentage of the asset. There are hundreds of great low-fee funds that charge expense ratios of 1 percent or less.

One way around the higher fees normally charged by employer-based plans: Make periodic partial rollovers from your 401(k) into an IRA (if your employer allows this). Shifting money from high-cost funds in a high-fee 401(k) plan into a fee-free IRA with lower cost investment options lets more of your money work for you. And if you have 401(k) accounts parked with old employers, roll them over ASAP to slash fees and supercharge investment options.

Chapter 4

Stretch Out Your Savings

Once you've retired, your number one financial focus will be making your money last. You can come at that from both sides: reducing expenses and optimizing investment returns. Since you have more control (though not total control) over spending than earnings, most people focus on minimizing expenses. However, that ignores the other side of the equation, and may lead you to *under*spend during retirement. Taking a balanced, both-sides approach can deliver a more enjoyable, financially secure retirement.

STAY INVESTED FOR THE LONG TERM

It's Just the Beginning

Financially speaking, retirement is not like crossing a finish line; it's more like handing off a baton in an ongoing relay race. You still have decades of time left, and your nest egg needs to last for all of them. Between inflation, higher-than-expected healthcare costs, and dozens of other potential budget busters, you need that nest egg to keep working for you. The only way it can do that is through investment growth and income. That's why you need to maintain a long-term investing strategy throughout your retirement, while making sure to carefully protect the money that will cover your shorter-term needs.

THE BUCKET STRATEGY

Employing a bucket strategy in retirement is one of the best ways to harness the power of growth investing without risking the cash you need in the near future. This method splits your nest egg into three distinct pieces: soon, later, and a long way off. In a nutshell, your "soon" bucket holds only 100 percent safety guaranteed cash; your "later" bucket holds extremely conservative income-producing investments; and the "long way off" bucket holds growth-focused investments. You can shift money between buckets on a set schedule or on an as-needed basis, depending on your overall situation and guaranteed income streams (such as Social Security and pension payments). Your financial advisor can help you figure out how much money to devote to each bucket and where to hold each depending on your overall financial situation.

Soon

The "soon" bucket covers the money you'll need for the next eighteen months to three years, the money you absolutely cannot afford to lose. The money in this bucket goes strictly into FDIC-insured bank accounts. You won't see earnings (other than minimal interest) here, but there will be no risk of losing even $1 to market forces. If you want to earn a little more interest than a typical bank or credit union offers, look into money market accounts (*not* money market funds) and online savings accounts. Online savings accounts typically offer slightly higher interest rates than brick-and-mortar banks. When this bucket holds less than eighteen months' worth of expenses, move some money into it from your "later" bucket.

Later

Your "later" bucket is for money you expect to need in the next three to five years (you can stretch that five years all the way up to ten years if you're risk-averse). You can afford a *little* more risk here in exchange for slightly higher earnings, but the focus is still safe preservation. The money in this bucket can be held in conservative money market funds, investment grade bond funds, and similar low-risk investments. If you have a very strong stomach or other income sources to rely on, you can minimize the amount in this bucket or invest a portion of it in dividend-paying blue-chip or preferred stock funds. When your "later" bucket starts to run low, transfer some money into it from your "long way off" bucket.

Long Way Off

The "long way off" bucket will hold money you don't expect to need for *at least* five years. The money in this bucket can stand more risk than the other two because there's time for recovery. You can invest this money for long-term growth (but think steady, rather than aggressive, growth). Good investment choices here include REITs (either individually or inside funds), low-cost broad stock market ETFs or index mutual funds, and, for possibly a small portion, higher-risk securities like international stock index funds.

CONSIDER RETIREMENT INCOME FUNDS

If you want steady income with more flexibility than you have with pensions and annuities, take a look at retirement income funds. While these mutual funds are *not guaranteed* like pensions and annuities, they can take all of the research, stress, and guesswork out of safe retirement investing. These all-in-one-funds invest your money for the primary purpose of producing monthly income and the secondary purpose of preserving principal. Like regular mutual funds, you have total control over when and how you access your money.

With an income and preservation (rather than growth) focus, the funds are very conservative. Typical annual returns average only around 3 percent to 4 percent, keeping pace with inflation without taking on any added risk.

Providing Monthly Income

Retirement income funds are all-in-one-funds that invest your money in a diversified portfolio of funds designed to produce income. They're sort of like target date funds in that they're actively managed mixed (stock and bond) funds, but they're different in their goals; here, income is the main priority. Most of the funds have target payout rates, ranging anywhere from 1 percent to 8 percent; the most common payout rate is 4 percent. Payout rates let you know how much money you'll receive as a percentage of your balance. For example, if you had a $1,000,000 fund balance and an annual payout rate of 4 percent, you'd receive $40,000 per year, or about $3,300 per month. Funds with higher listed payout rates typically hold a larger proportion of stocks funds (to sustain those rates long-term) than those with lower rates.

Be aware that because these are not guaranteed funds, monthly income and fund value will vary based on market conditions, and both could decline dramatically.

What to Look for in Retirement Income Funds

With more than 300 retirement income funds on the market, it can be tough to know which to choose. Here are the most important factors to consider:

- The fund's long-term (meaning at least five or ten years) returns
- Low expense ratios (0.5 percent or less; especially important with modest returns)
- Sales loads (look for no-load funds)

You can find retirement income funds that match these criteria with online fund-finding tools, available on sites like *Morningstar* (www.morningstar.com) and *Reuters* (www.reuters.com).

Vanguard (www.vanguard.com), Fidelity (www.fidelity.com), and Charles Schwab (www.schwab.com) all offer funds that meet these requirements.

Separate the Rates

Don't confuse the fund's payout rate (the money you receive) with its rate of return (the fund's annual earnings). The retirement income fund you choose may not earn enough in any given year to cover the payout rate. When that happens, some of your monthly income payment might be a return of principal, reducing future earnings and payout potential.

INCLUDE YOUR OTHER INCOME SOURCES

Everything Counts

Your retirement income will come from other sources in addition to your retirement savings. You'll get some money from Social Security. Many people have some money stockpiled in nonretirement savings and investment accounts. You may also turn to a part-time job or consulting gigs to supplement your monthly income.

WORKING IN RETIREMENT

More than just another source of income, working in some capacity during retirement offers social benefits and a sense of purpose. Continuing to work doesn't have to mean sticking with the same job you've had—especially if you were more than ready to say goodbye to it. Millions of retirees embark on "encore" careers, either offshoots of what they'd done before or pursuits of a lifelong passion.

Whatever you decide about working, you also get to decide your preferred time investment, whether that's part-time, seasonal, sporadic, or full-time. Any work you do brings in more income, helping you pull less from your retirement nest egg. Depending on your age and work situation, you may be able to contribute more money toward retirement, delay taking RMDs, or build up nonretirement-account assets.

Boost Retirement Savings

Just because you're old enough to be retired doesn't mean you're not working. And if you're working, you may still be able to contribute to tax-advantaged retirement accounts. There are three basic options here:

1. **Roth IRA:** As long as you have earned income (below the IRS phase-out limit), you can continue to put money into a Roth IRA for as long as you want, up to that year's maximum contribution.
2. **Employer-sponsored plans:** If your employer offers a 401(k) or 403(b) retirement plan, you can keep contributing regardless of your age; plus you don't have to take any RMDs from that plan until you stop working there.
3. **SEP-IRA:** If you're self-employed, you can contribute to a SEP-IRA (details on these in Chapter 3) no matter how old you are. However, you will have to start taking RMDs after you reach age seventy-and-a-half (yes, that means you'd be both contributing and withdrawing in the same year).

Any of these can help you stash more cash and spend your savings more slowly, adding an extra layer of security to your retirement.

You Can Stop Social Security (Maybe)

If you decide to go back to work but are already collecting Social Security retirement benefits, you may be able to stop them. How this works depends on your current age and how long ago you started taking benefits.

If you've already reached your full retirement age (sixty-seven for anyone born in or after 1960), you can suspend your Social Security benefits until you reach age seventy. To do this, you need to notify the Social Security Administration (SSA) verbally (by calling 1-800-772-1213), in person at your local office, or in writing; you can't make this request online. You can go back to collecting benefits at any time by notifying the SSA that you've changed your mind.

If you haven't yet reached your full retirement age, you can withdraw your Social Security claim as long as it hasn't been longer than one year and as long as you haven't withdrawn before (you can only do it once). In this case, you have to repay all of the benefits you (and your family) have received based on that original claim. To withdraw from the program, you'll need to fill out and submit Form SSA 521, which is available on their website at www.ssa.gov. They'll notify you when your request has been approved (or not), and let you know how much you owe them.

SET UP MULTIPLE RELIABLE INCOME STREAMS

The number one rule of retirement: Make sure to have more than one reliable source of future income. Social Security retirement benefits may be the foundation of your income, but most people will need more than that to cover even basic monthly expenses. If you're not one of the lucky few with a guaranteed pension, you'll need to set up reliable income streams on your own. Sounds hard, but it's actually pretty straightforward. The key here is to trade risk and growth for wealth preservation and steady income.

Build a Bond Ladder

Bonds are loans that bondholders (investors) make to corporations or governments. Just like any other loan, bonds come with specific interest rates, payment terms, and due dates (known as maturity dates). During the life of the bond, bondholders usually get semi-annual fixed interest payments (though some bonds pay interest more or less frequently). When the bond matures (comes due), the bondholder gets back the entire loan amount (called face value).

A bond ladder refers to a collection of individual bonds (not bond funds) with varying maturity dates that sync up with your future expected cash needs. Bond maturities can range from six months to thirty years. You can build a bond ladder that results in one bond coming due every year for thirty years, or look at your retirement budget to see where bigger than usual expenses might crop up.

Some factors to consider when you're buying individual bonds for income security:

- Choose only investment-grade bonds with credit ratings no lower than BBB–.
- Consider each bond's tax characteristics (i.e., taxable or tax-exempt).
- Avoid *callable* bonds, which can be cashed out before their stated maturity dates.

You can learn more about investing in bonds at www.kiplinger .com. Bonds are a little more difficult to select and buy than stocks, so consider working with your financial advisor to create your bond ladder.

Buy an Immediate Annuity

Annuities (which are discussed in detail in Chapter 8) can get very complicated and expensive. At their most basic, though, annuities provide guaranteed income streams, just like pensions. An immediate annuity starts providing that guaranteed income right away. This will be money you can rely on, just like Social Security, so you don't have to worry about whether you can pay your bills.

Once you retire, consider taking a portion of your nest egg and converting it into an *immediate fixed* annuity. You can buy a term annuity that guarantees payments for a fixed period of time (such as ten years) or a lifetime annuity. Like any investment (though technically these are insurance products and not investments), annuities come with drawbacks and potential risks. For one thing, you need to hand over a sizeable chunk of cash, which can limit liquidity. Also, you and your spouse may lose money if you die soon after buying a lifetime annuity or before the final payment of a term annuity; this depends on the details of the specific annuity contract.

Rental Real Estate

Rental real estate can provide stable income that keeps pace with inflation. Whether you want to be a hands-on landlord or a hands-off investor, rental real estate can make a great post-retirement investment choice.

If you decide to go the landlord route, make sure you know what you're getting into. Getting started in rental properties calls for a big initial cash infusion. Plus, you'll have ongoing expenses for the property, and constant reliable tenants are never guaranteed. This option can work well for people with a DIY home improvement, contractor, or handyman background, as well as for real estate professionals. If you like the idea of owning physical real estate but don't have experience with rentals, work with an experienced, trustworthy property manager; it will decrease your income stream, but more than make up for it in hassle reduction.

REITs (real estate investment trusts) offer many of the same benefits without any of the difficulties that come with being a landlord. In exchange for special tax treatment, REITs are *required* to distribute at least 90 percent of their taxable income every year. You can invest in REITs through ETFs and mutual funds (allowing for a more diversified REIT portfolio), or purchase shares of publicly traded REITs (which are subject to market volatility) just like you would buy individual stocks. You can learn more about REITs by visiting Nareit (National Association of Real Estate Investment Trusts) at www.reit.com.

Income from Dozens of Properties

REITs are sort of like mutual funds, but instead of stocks or bonds they hold portfolios of commercial or residential rental properties. Typically, each REIT specializes in a single type of property, such as office buildings or hotels. They take on all of the property management hassles and pay the income to investors.

SAFE WITHDRAWAL STRATEGIES

Protect Your Principal

It can be difficult to figure out how much of your money you can "safely" spend each year. With so many unknown variables floating around, you can never know for sure what your financial picture might look like from one year to the next. Your best bet is to focus on what you do know—how much money you have today, how much money you need (for essential, rather than optional, spending) this year, how long you expect to live, and your guaranteed income sources. That combination of factors is your starting point for making decisions about withdrawals that won't leave you struggling now or stranded later.

THREE BASIC STRATEGIES

There are several "rule of thumb" retirement withdrawal strategies recommended by financial advisors. Any of these basic plans help you withdraw money in a way that offers a good chance that you won't run out of money. Use these as guidelines rather than strict rules. Retirement lasts a long time, and what works in the first few years may not work in the future. Keep your strategy firm but flexible, so you'll be in the strongest possible financial position.

The 4 Percent Rule

The withdrawal strategy that is most often talked about is known as the 4 percent rule. By keeping at least 50 percent of your retirement portfolio invested in stocks and the balance in bonds, you'd most likely be able to withdraw 4 percent (adjusted for inflation) of your money annually for at least thirty years. That 4 percent rate has worked even during nasty market downturns.

The strategy works like this: In your first year of retirement, you withdraw 4 percent of your savings. For example, if you had a $500,000 nest egg, you'd withdraw $20,000 during year one. The next year, you'd adjust that $20,000 for inflation. For example, if inflation was 2.4 percent in retirement year two, you'd withdraw $20,480 ($20,000 × 1.024). Every year, you'd withdraw the prior year's amount plus the inflation adjustment. Though this method is not guaranteed (no method is), as long as at least 50 percent of your retirement nest egg remains invested in stocks, there's a strong chance that you won't run out of money.

Rocket Science and Soda

The 4 percent method, also known as the "Bengen rule," was dreamed up by financial advisor William Bengen back in 1994. What most people don't know is that Bengen started out as a rocket scientist, then worked as the chief operating officer of his family's soda-bottling company before switching gears to become a certified financial planner.

Percentage of Portfolio

With this drawdown method, every year you withdraw a fixed percentage of your nest egg based on the prior year's ending balance. This strategy allows for smaller withdrawals during down years, which increases the likelihood that you won't use up your money too quickly. On the flip side, it allows for greater withdrawals when the portfolio is performing well, which can help fund vacations, hobbies, and other entertainment.

Many people, however, have a hard time living with the uncertainty attached to this method. Since this year's withdrawals are based on last year's portfolio performance, it's harder to manage a budget or make sure you have all of your essential expenses covered. So, while this is a very good idea from a portfolio preservation perspective, it really only works for people who have other ways to cover their expenses in down years. Another potential downside: In down years, the percentage may not be as much as the RMD, which can knock the strategy off course.

The Essential Expense Method

The essential expense method (sometimes called the income floor method) calls for making sure all of your essential expenses are covered by guaranteed income streams, such as Social Security, pensions, and annuities. This helps ensure that you won't be backed into a corner and forced to sell off retirement account holdings when the market is down. When those expenses are covered, you can use your RMDs for the fun stuff; if your retirement nest egg is in Roth IRA accounts, you don't have to make any withdrawals at all unless you want to.

To use this strategy, total up your essential monthly expenses. Essential expenses include only absolute necessities, like housing, food, medicine, and transportation. Next, add up your total guaranteed income sources. If they're enough to cover those essential expenses, you can stop right there. If not, you can boost your guaranteed income stream with options such as an immediate fixed annuity or a bond ladder.

THE DYNAMIC SPENDING MODEL

If you don't want to be locked into your annual withdrawal amount regardless of circumstances, you might prefer a dynamic spending model. This strategy doesn't rigidly adhere to a particular percentage or dollar value every year and offers a better chance that your money will last longer. It employs a combination of both percentage-of-portfolio withdrawals and fixed-dollar spending, allowing you to be responsive to market conditions without enduring huge swings in income from year to year. This method is a little more complicated to set up, so you might want to consider consulting a financial advisor. You can find a good example of this strategy (with numbers) at www.vanguardblog.com.

Basically, with this method, you set minimums and maximums for your annual withdrawals, so you always know your income range. In flush years, you can spend more. In down years, you'll still cover expenses without hurting your nest egg. You start by coming up with your ideal spending rate, the amount you'd like to withdraw every year (a lot of people stick with 4 percent here). Then you determine a maximum percentage (the amount you'd like to add to last year's spending if the markets do well) and a minimum percentage (the amount you'd be able to cut from last year's spending if it is a down year).

Each year, you figure out your current base spending amount (your spending rate multiplied by last year's ending portfolio balance). For example, if your spending rate was 4 percent and the portfolio balance was $500,000, your base spending amount would be $20,000 ($500,000 × 0.04). Next, you figure out your minimum and maximum based on *last year's* base spending amount. For example, if your maximum spending rate is 10 percent more than last year, you would multiply last year's base amount by 1.10. If your minimum spending rate is 5 percent less than last year, you would multiply last year's base amount by 0.95.

If this year's base amount is greater than the maximum, you withdraw the maximum. If your base amount is less than your minimum, you withdraw the minimum. And if it falls between the two, you just withdraw your base amount that year.

DOWNSIZE FIXED EXPENSES

Honey, I Shrunk the Budget

Cutting your fixed expenses is one of the best ways to improve your retirement cash flow. Fixed expenses are the costs you pay the same amount every month. The more fixed expenses you have, the more retirement income you'll need to cover them. That can result in a faster drawdown than you were expecting, which both runs through the money faster and reduces potential portfolio earnings and growth. By reducing the expenses you can control, you'll have more flexibility when unexpected expenses crop up.

HOUSING

Housing costs are almost always the biggest expenses retirees face. That can be a huge problem, especially for people who rely primarily on Social Security for income. Consider this: The average monthly Social Security check is $1,461, and the average monthly housing costs for retirees (according to the US Bureau of Labor Statistics) are $1,322. That leaves less than $200 to cover everything else!

Even if your mortgage is paid off (or close to it), there are still many other costs that will never disappear, including the following:

- Property taxes
- Homeowners insurance
- Utilities
- Repairs and maintenance

With large or older houses, those costs can run very high for homeowners. On the rental side, the average rent for a one-bedroom apartment in the United States costs $1,140 per month (according to the 2019 Annual Rent Guide by www.apartmentguide.com), but rents run almost double that in higher-cost-of-living areas. Bottom line: In retirement, housing will be your biggest *controllable* expense, and decreasing your housing costs will go a long way toward stretching your savings.

Go Smaller

When you move into a smaller, less expensive home, your mortgage or rent payment isn't the only cost you'll cut: Virtually all of your other home-related expenses will shrink as well. Here are just a few of the ways you'll save money by downsizing your home:

- Lower heating and cooling costs
- Smaller insurance premiums
- Lower property taxes (yes, renters pay these, too, just not directly)
- Lower maintenance costs
- Reduced cleaning costs (whether you use a housekeeper or your own cleaning supplies)

On top of all that, a smaller place will be much easier to take care of every day.

Cut the Cost of Living

If you're willing and able to relocate, you may be able to substantially cut your cost of living (COL), starting with your rent or mortgage payment. In lower COL areas, you'll save on almost everything, from food to utilities to fun activities. Check out these astounding average price differences for everyday items in four US cities (from www.bankrate.com):

ITEM	AKRON, OH	PHOENIX, AZ	NEW HAVEN, CT	BOISE, ID
Dozen eggs	$1.87	$2.12	$3.10	$1.86
Dentist visit	$73.53	$98.67	$111.48	$87.20
Gallon of gas	$2.34	$2.49	$2.52	$2.47
Half-gallon of milk	$2.74	$1.73	$3.39	$1.76
Apartment rent	$766.67	$880.33	$1,355.00	$699.50

There's one more big issue to consider when you're looking at COL: taxes. Moving to a tax-friendly state can make a huge difference to your after-tax income. Many states exclude retirement income from taxes, a couple of states tax only interest and dividends, and seven states charge no income tax at all. You can find a "Retiree Tax Map" of the US on the Kiplinger website (www.kiplinger.com).

LOAN PAYMENTS

Debt plagues the vast majority of Americans. No matter what type of debt you're carrying, paying it off before you retire is one of the best financial moves you can make—that's especially true if you have high-interest debt (such as a personal loan or credit card balances). Not only do loan payments eat into your retirement income, they also come with interest, sometimes at a higher rate than your portfolio could possibly earn. Aggressively tackling debt while you're still working or as soon as possible after you stop working is the best sure-thing high-return investment you can make.

Don't Borrow from Retirement Savings

You'll do more damage to your overall financial picture if you pull money out of retirement accounts (before retirement) to pay down debt. First, you'll have to pay tax on the money you take out (unless it's a proper withdrawal from a Roth IRA account), which reduces the amount of the debt paydown. Second, if it's an early withdrawal (made before age fifty-nine-and-a-half), you'll have to pay the IRS a penalty of an extra 10 percent. Third, you'll lose all the future compounding that money could have earned, which could amount to hundreds of thousands of dollars (depending on your age and investments).

Borrowing from your 401(k) isn't much better, and it comes with its own set of potential pitfalls. For example, you have to start paying that loan back with your next paycheck, which often results in more credit card spending. Plus, if you leave your job for any reason, the loan has to be paid back in full. Just like with an early withdrawal, you'll also lose compounding power—even more so if your employer doesn't allow contributions to the 401(k) while you have an outstanding loan. Either way, this isn't the best choice for paying down debt.

Pay Down Debt Strategically

Paying off debt is hard. It calls for some temporary sacrifices (like making extreme budget cuts or working a second job), but being debt-free is worth it. There are different ways to tackle debt, but if you want the fastest way, start with your highest-interest-rate debt. That's because you'll pay less money overall, which allows you to make bigger payments on other debt going forward. If you're not sure which has the highest interest rate, make a list of all of your outstanding debt.

Include the current balance, monthly or minimum payment amount, payment due date, and interest rate for each debt. Then rank each debt according to the rate, from highest to lowest. For debt that is not from credit cards, make sure you specifically indicate that extra payments are to be used to pay down principal. For credit card debt, you can decrease interest charges further and faster by making two or more payments throughout the month. Credit cards calculate debt based on average daily balances, so making at least one partial payment early in the month has the effect of lowering the average daily balance, resulting in a smaller interest charge.

INSURANCE

When you add up all the different policies you carry, the amount you're spending on insurance every year may surprise you. This expense serves an important financial purpose: protecting you against extreme losses if they occur. Every time you don't use insurance, it might feel like you're throwing money away; but when you do need it, you'll be glad it's there. The trick is walking the line between inadequate insurance coverage and coverage that is much higher than the property insured; that line is different for everyone based on their personal situation. Revisit all of your insurance policies to make sure you aren't paying for coverage you don't need or overpaying for the coverage you do need. Adjusting your policies can reduce your fixed expenses in a way you'll rarely (if ever) notice.

Health Insurance

Downsizing your health insurance isn't about cutting back on coverage; it's about making sure you have the best coverage for your and your family's healthcare needs. Saving money by slashing premiums could wind up costing you more in deductibles, copays, and other out-of-pocket costs if you use a lot of healthcare services. If you have health insurance through an employer, read through all of the options before you choose a plan. Don't just stick with the plan you had last year, especially if your family or health situation has changed. If you're buying insurance on the marketplace (www .healthcare.gov), use the plan preview option to see your personalized costs before you lock into a plan.

Car Insurance

If you haven't looked at your car insurance policy in a while, this is the perfect time to make sure you have the right amount of coverage and are taking advantage of every possible discount. See if it makes sense to lower your deductibles (especially if you've recently had a young or accident-prone driver on the policy). Shop around to see if another company offers better rates; you might be able to save hundreds of (even a thousand) dollars a year for the same coverage. You can find an in-depth look at comparing car insurance premiums at NerdWallet (www.nerdwallet.com).

Homeowners/Renters Insurance

The amount you pay for home insurance can vary by hundreds of dollars per year depending on your coverage and the company you choose. Aside from increasing deductibles or bundling home and auto policies to reduce premiums, here are some more ways to lower your home insurance costs:

- Insure the value of the house itself, not the price you paid for it, which includes land.
- Beef up home security to both protect your valuables and score policy discounts.
- Match your coverage with a current asset inventory to make sure they still mesh.
- Check your insurer for little-known discounts (like having fire extinguishers in the home, living close to a fire station, or keeping your trees trimmed).
- Improve your credit score (yes, insurers can factor this into policy pricing).

Like with other types of insurance, it makes sense to shop around for your home insurance policy, especially if you're using a different company to insure your car.

Cut Back Nonessentials

You may have more fixed expenses than you even realize, especially if you use auto-pay for recurring expenses like cable and Internet, streaming services, gym memberships, and subscription services. These nonessential expenses, which pay for services that you may not even be using, can drain a sizeable chunk of your monthly budget. Go through bank and credit card statements to sniff out these extra budget busters.

AVOID THESE SPENDING TRAPS

Budget Quicksand

It's easy for recent retirees to fall into spending traps, especially when they're not yet used to the way money flows without the regular paycheck they were used to. While you want to make sure to enjoy your time, it's crucial to keep an eye on your financial situation and stick with the budget you've made (which should absolutely include room for fun).

Focusing on fun at the expenses of finances can deplete your savings at an unsustainable clip and derail your retirement security. Try to avoid common spending traps to keep your retirement fully funded and free from anxiety about money.

BUYING—AND KEEPING— STUFF YOU DON'T NEED

Many retirees go on spending sprees when they first stop working and their retirement accounts are full. They splurge on vacations, home renovations, sports equipment, and club memberships now that they finally have plenty of free time to enjoy themselves. But overspending in those early years—especially if you haven't budgeted for those extra expenditures—can create a bigger hole in your retirement nest egg than you realize.

Watch Your "Fun Stuff" Spending

Retirement is a time to indulge in fun, but that doesn't mean you have to buy a lot of stuff. Many retirees plunk down a chunk of cash for new sporting equipment or big-ticket items (like boats) because they've "always wanted to..." Before you bust your budget to buy a new set of golf clubs, fishing gear, or an RV, try renting or borrowing first. You may not like an activity as much as you think you will, even if it's something you loved doing years ago. Plus, those big-ticket items (like boats and RVs) come with ongoing expenses, like registration, storage, insurance, gas, and maintenance costs.

Once you've tried out the activity and decided you want to pursue it, it still may be more cost-effective to rent. To see if buying is *really* worth it, add up the cost of the item plus a few years' worth of any ongoing expenses. Next, divide that by the number of times you realistically will use the item. Compare that per-use cost to the cost of renting the item, which is often much less expensive than buying the item in the long run.

Too Many Cars?

After retirement, does your family really need to keep more than one car? If there's not a specific reason you're holding on to a second car, this is a good time to get rid of it. Whether you donate it, sell it, or gift it to a child or grandchild, you'll save a lot of money by sticking with a single car. You'll trim several ongoing expenses from your budget, including:

- Insurance
- Registration fees
- Gas
- Repairs and maintenance

Plus, if you sell the car, you'll get an instant cash infusion that you can either throw into savings or use instead of pulling more cash from retirement funds. If you donate it, you could score a sizeable tax deduction (if you itemize deductions) and reduce your income tax bill—another big money saver.

DON'T TAKE ON NEW DEBT

According to the National Council on Aging, around 60 percent of seniors carry debt into retirement, with an average debt load of $31,300. On top of that, many retirees take on new debt, putting their future financial security at an even higher risk. Before you sign on the dotted line to take on a new loan, especially if it's not for yourself, talk with a trusted financial advisor about other options.

Avoid Cosigning Loans

It's becoming increasingly common for parents (and grandparents) to cosign for everything from student loans to apartment leases. Helping your child (or grandchild) start to build credit and have access to things they wouldn't have on their own might seem like a good idea. The problems start when they stop making payments—something that happens around 40 percent of the time.

When you cosign for a loan or credit card, you are 100 percent responsible for making payments if the other borrower can't or doesn't. Not only are you on the hook financially, but all of the credit black marks show up on your credit report as well, which can make it harder or more expensive for you to borrow money for yourself. Plus, depending on the specific circumstances, your wages could be garnished, shrinking your retirement budget even further.

Use Caution with Home Equity Loans

Many people take out home equity loans when they're having trouble making ends meet. After all, homes are often the largest asset people have, and it's very easy to borrow against the equity. That seems like a great idea when home values are high or growing, but the real estate market can turn on a dime (like we saw in 2008). If that happens, you could suddenly owe more money than your home is worth (be "underwater" on the loan). That might not be a huge issue if you're planning on staying in the house for a long time, but it can cripple your finances if you need to sell before the market rebounds. Remember, with home equity loans, if you can't keep up with the payments, you could lose your home.

Renovate Wisely

Many new retirees take on home renovation projects, which often leads to taking out home equity loans. Before you start, make sure the renovations you choose will add value to your life and to your home price. Renovations that include making repairs or adding a deck almost always add value; upgrading to top-of-the-line appliances usually doesn't add value.

Chapter 5

Plan for the Biggest Retirement Expenses

When it comes to estimating retirement expenses, people often go too low on the "big five" costs: healthcare, taxes, housing, transportation and travel, and caring for family. That can lead to undersaving for retirement and overspending in the earlier years. To make sure you've got it covered, take extra care when budgeting for the biggest retirement expenses. Most of your savings will be spent in these five categories, so making a plan to control these costs before they wipe out your nest egg is critical to your future financial security. This is a good time to call in a financial advisor, particularly one who has extensive experience with retirement planning, so you don't overlook something that can tip the balance toward running out of money.

HEALTHCARE

Inoculate Your Savings

Most people never talk about healthcare costs with their financial advisors, but it's often the single biggest expense throughout retirement—even for relatively healthy people. The average senior couple should expect to spend about $285,000 in out-of-pocket healthcare costs (according to Fidelity), which includes insurance premiums. And if you happen to be among the nearly 80 percent of adults with at least one chronic healthcare issue (such as arthritis or high blood pressure), you'll almost certainly spend more. On top of that, around 70 percent of retirees eventually need some form of long-term care, which can add (on average) $250,000 to those out-of-pocket costs. That's why it's critical to include healthcare costs in your financial planning.

HOW TO ESTIMATE FUTURE HEALTHCARE COSTS

It's impossible to predict your future healthcare costs with absolute accuracy. However, you can come up with the most reasonable estimate based on specific factors about your personal and family medical history and your expected longevity. Start with your expected Medicare premiums, which typically start at age sixty-five, by visiting www.medicare.gov. You'll also want to account for the costs of chronic illnesses, regular medications, and wellness activities that already affect your budget. Finally, factor in the way you use healthcare to come up with a realistic estimate to use in your retirement budget.

What's Your Medical Spending Style?

One of the most important factors for accurately estimating your future healthcare costs involves how you use healthcare today. Some people avoid going to doctors and dentists until they're so sick or injured there's no other choice. Other people go to the doctor every time they feel something coming on. Knowing the amount of healthcare services you use now informs your estimate of future medical expenses.

Another point to consider: Do you spend more on *well* care or *sick* care? People who get regular exams and screenings may be able to prevent or slow disease progression, while people who don't focus on prevention could eventually experience much more advanced chronic conditions that are harder (and more expensive) to treat.

Genetic Testing

Genetic tests help predict your chances of developing health problems and how well you'll respond to various treatment options if you do become ill. When you know you face a high probability of developing a disease, you can work with your doctor to take recommended steps to reduce your risk factors.

Family and Personal Health History

You can do a lot to keep yourself healthier, but you can't change your genes (at least not yet). Your family medical history, including your personal healthcare history, offers substantial clues to your future medical spending needs. You can plug in the specifics to the free online American Association of Retired Persons (AARP) Healthcare Costs Calculator (www.aarp.org) to get a personalized estimate, including what portion of expenses could be covered by Medicare and how much you'll have to pay out of pocket.

LONG-TERM CARE COVERAGE

Regular disability and health insurance policies—and that includes Medicare—do not cover the long-term care services people need when they're struck by a chronic disease or disability. Those services include assistance with daily activities like getting dressed, whether you're living at home, in a nursing home, or at an assisted-living facility. Around half of all people age sixty-five and older will need those services at some point, even if it's just for a few years. The annual costs of long-term care can be staggering, ranging from around $20,000 (for adult daycare) to $50,000 for in-home care to around $100,000 (to stay in a nursing home), and paying for it falls solely on your shoulders. If you run out of money entirely, Medicaid steps in—and that program typically covers only nursing home care from facilities that will accept Medicaid payments.

That's where long-term care coverage comes in. Not only can this insurance protect your savings, it also gives you better options when it comes to the quality of care. You can only buy these policies while you're in good health, so they're usually purchased by adults aged forty-five to sixty. Unfortunately, premiums can be expensive (though less costly than paying for long-term care), and there are few companies that offer these policies.

The Cost

Though rates for long-term care coverage vary greatly depending on several factors, they're all pretty expensive. According to the American Association for Long-Term Care Insurance (AALTCI), the average annual cost of a policy for a single fifty-five-year-old man is $2,050, for a single fifty-five-year-old woman is $2,700, and for a fifty-five-year-old couple combined is $3,050. That's not really surprising when you consider the costs they're expected to cover for years or even decades, but it does make it harder to afford. Plus, premiums may go up after you've purchased a policy, if state regulators approve the rate hike (which they probably will if the cost of claims increases).

Premiums depend on a variety of factors, including:

- Age
- State of health
- Gender
- Coverage options (daily and lifetime limits, cost of living adjustments, elimination periods)
- Insurance company

Age is one of the biggest factors here. Buying a long-term care policy when you're younger (before age sixty) will cost less per year than waiting until age sixty-five or longer. Plus, the longer you wait, the more likely you won't be able to get coverage based on health status.

Keeping the coverage simple can reduce the cost. Most people do okay with getting enough coverage for a few years of home healthcare, and going with a lower percentage of inflation protection (choosing 1 percent instead of 3 percent, for example).

Prices for coverage vary among insurance companies, so compare quotes before making any decisions. You can buy directly from most companies or through an insurance agent; for this type of insurance, talking with an experienced independent insurance broker who works with multiple carriers will help you find the right policy at the right price.

How It Works

Long-term care policies kick in when you can no longer perform at least two of six basic activities of daily living (ADLs) by yourself. Those activities include:

- Getting in and out of bed or chairs (called transferring)
- Getting on or off the toilet (called toileting)
- Bathing
- Getting dressed
- Eating
- Dealing with incontinence

The claims process starts when you need this level of care. The insurance company will look at detailed documents from your doctor and may set up an evaluation with a nurse. If they agree that you need this help, they'll look at your care plan. If they approve that "plan of care," coverage will kick in after an "elimination period" (usually one, two, or three months); after that, you'll start receiving reimbursement for costs. Most policies will cover only up to a daily limit and only until you reach the lifetime limit. Those limits vary by policy, and figure in to the premium costs.

Other Ways to Manage Long-Term Care Costs

If you're priced out of long-term care coverage or can't get coverage for some reason, there are still some things you can do to avoid relying on Medicaid if you run out of money. Here are a few other ways to get long-term care insurance coverage:

- **Cover yourself:** Set up your own long-term care fund to cover three to five years' worth of in-home healthcare services, approximately $150,000 to $250,000, preferably in an HSA (health savings account).
- **Tap into life insurance:** Many permanent (whole life) insurance policies offer the chance to tap into future death benefits to pay for long-term care.
- **Buy an immediate fixed annuity:** Regardless of your age or health status, you can buy an immediate fixed annuity to supply a steady stream of future income, and you can use that cash to pay or offset long-term care costs.

Odds are that you or your spouse (maybe both) will require long-term care coverage at some point. Make sure you have some way to cover those very high costs.

TAXES

Avoid but Don't Evade

People tend to overlook taxes when they're figuring out their retirement expenses, but it's one of the biggest. Depending on where you live and what kinds of things you do, you'll pay income tax, property tax, sales tax, gas tax, hotel occupancy tax, and many more. Sometimes you may not even realize you're paying taxes, but they all add up and can suck up a large chunk out of your monthly cash. Here, we'll focus on federal income taxes, and all the new rules and issues you'll need to deal with once you reach retirement age.

DON'T SKIP YOUR RMDS

RMDs (required minimum distributions) are just what they sound like: The least amount of money you *must* withdraw from qualified retirement accounts every year once you reach age seventy-and-a-half. If you don't, you'll be subject to a 50 percent penalty on the RMD you didn't take plus any regular income taxes.

Qualified retirement accounts include the following:

- Traditional IRAs
- 401(k) plans
- 403(b) plans
- 457 plans
- SEP-IRAs

There is an exception: If you're still working for an employer (and don't own 5 percent or more of the company), you don't have to take RMDs from *that* employer's 401(k) plan. However, you still have to take RMDs from any other 401(k) accounts you have.

You Can Take More

There's a lot of confusion surrounding RMDs. One of the most common questions is "What if I need more than that?" RMDs represent the *smallest* withdrawal you can make. There are no restrictions on taking more; no maximum distribution limits.

How to Calculate Your RMD

To figure out how much money you have to withdraw from your retirement accounts each year, you need to know two numbers:

1. The total balance of your retirement accounts (excluding Roth IRAs) as of December 31 of the prior year
2. The IRS distribution period

For the second piece, head over to the IRS website (www.irs .gov) and look at IRS Publication 590. This publication includes an RMD worksheet and the life expectancy tables used to make the calculations. Find your age on the Uniform Lifetime Table and the corresponding distribution period in the next column. Divide your retirement account balance by the distribution period to get your RMD for the year.

Here's an example: Let's say you are age seventy-eight and had $400,000 in RMD-required retirement accounts as of December 31 last year. According to the IRS life expectancy table, your distribution period is 20.3. Divide $400,000 by 20.3 to get your RMD of $19,705 for this year ($400,000 / 20.3 = $19,705). You can take that in one lump sum or a bunch of payments throughout the year. You can take it all from one account or a portion from multiple accounts. As long as you withdraw at least $19,705, you won't face any IRS penalties.

Married Couples Keep It Separate

If you and your spouse each have retirement accounts in your own names, you'll have to figure out your RMDs separately and pull them from your own accounts. A lot of couples get in trouble with the IRS by withdrawing their total joint RMDs from one spouse's account, figuring it's all the same if they file a joint tax return. That can result in big IRS fines, charged to the spouse whose account went untouched, since that spouse technically did not take an RMD.

THE FOUR-STEP PLAN TO MINIMIZE YOUR TAX BILL

As soon as you start taking money out of your retirement accounts (except for Roth IRAs), federal and (possibly) state income taxes will come into play. These income taxes will put a serious dent in your budget. You can minimize your income tax bill and preserve more of your retirement nest egg by making your withdrawals strategically using this four-step plan. Not only will this plan keep your income tax bill to the bare minimum, it may also help you avoid being taxed on your Social Security retirement benefits by carefully managing your taxable income.

1. Take your full RMD, whether or not you need it. Pulling this money first ensures you won't be hit with huge IRS penalties. Remember, just because you withdraw this money doesn't mean you have to spend it. You can put that cash into your emergency fund or into a regular taxable investment account where it can continue to work for you.

2. Take money out of your regular taxable investment accounts. The earnings in these accounts get taxed no matter what you do. Since you're already paying tax on those earnings, it won't increase your tax bill to withdraw them to use for your monthly expenses. If you need more than the available earnings and have to start selling investments, start with those that you've held for longer than one year to pay the least capital gains taxes.

3. Take money out of tax-free accounts (Roth IRAs). Do this only when the combination of RMDs and money from taxable accounts isn't enough to cover your regular monthly expenses. Since this money doesn't count as taxable income, it won't increase your tax bill. Plus, it helps you avoid paying any (or higher) taxes on Social Security benefits or higher Medicare premiums.

4. Take another withdrawal from your tax-deferred accounts, like traditional IRAs and 401(k) accounts, if you still need additional funds. This will increase your taxable income, but will also lower the amount you'll be required to withdraw for future RMDs.

When *Not* to Follow the Plan

That four-step plan makes sense when your goal is to minimize taxes, but in other circumstances it may not be the best strategy. For example, if your goal is to preserve tax-free growth and the highest possible amount of tax-free income in the future, swap steps three and four, leaving your Roth IRA accounts intact for as long as possible.

Another time to switch things up: You have a major unexpected expense and need to withdraw more money than expected. That extra draw could result in higher Medicare premiums and higher taxes on Social Security benefits, a situation that's better to avoid. If that expense is health-related, use money from an HSA before tapping into any other asset pools. For other big expenses (such as a major home repair), take the money from regular taxable accounts unless that would force you to sell short-term investments and trigger a bigger tax bill. In that case, take the money from a Roth IRA account to keep your taxable income as low as possible.

Taxes on Social Security Benefits

Your Social Security retirement benefits may be partially taxable depending on your other income. This starts with an income test. First, add all of your other income (including tax-exempt interest, which may be earned on certain bonds, for example) to half of your Social Security retirement benefits. If that total is more than your "base amount" (listed in IRS Publication 915), you'll have to pay taxes on at least 50 percent of your Social Security benefits. Higher income taxpayers may be taxed on up to 85 percent of those benefits.

MAKING ESTIMATED TAX PAYMENTS

When you're no longer earning a paycheck, you're also not prepaying your tax bill through employer withholding. That means you are now responsible for making those tax payments based on the amount of taxable income you expect to receive. If you underestimate, you may be subject to tax penalties (even if you pay on time), so it's important to use a realistic income estimate. The IRS also doles out penalties for late estimated payments, so you could owe penalties even if you get a tax refund.

Add Up Expected Income and Deductions

In your first year of retirement, figuring out estimated taxes is tricky because you don't really know what your cash flow will look like; it gets easier moving forward. Start with the numbers you know, such as your total RMDs for the whole year, guaranteed pension payments, and any steady employment income. If you have investments in regular (nonretirement) accounts, include any income you expect them to earn (like interest and dividends), using last year's earnings as a guide. Don't include any nontaxable income like withdrawals from Roth IRAs or loan proceeds.

Your safest bet when figuring deductions is to go with the standard deduction. If you do decide to itemize your deductions, you'll have less taxable income and a lower tax bill, so you won't have underpaid. You may also be able to deduct other things like student loan interest you paid and half of any self-employment taxes you paid.

If you're really worried about your estimate, use the IRS "safe harbor" rules as your guide. You can avoid tax penalties by making sure to pay at least 100 percent of last year's total tax bill or 90 percent of this year's tax bill, whichever is smaller. High-income taxpayers must pay at least 110 percent of last year's taxes to achieve safe harbor.

Calculate Your Estimated Tax Bill

Once you know your estimated taxable income, you can figure out your estimated income tax bill. To do it yourself, get Form 1040-ES from the IRS website (www.irs.gov). This publication includes a worksheet, detailed instructions, and the current year's tax tables. If you used tax prep software for your last year's income tax return, it can probably generate estimated tax payment amounts and payment coupons for you.

Keep in mind that if you're earning any self-employment income (from consulting, for example), you may also be on the hook for Social Security and Medicare taxes (collectively called self-employment taxes). Also remember to deduct any taxes that have been withheld from income you received (for example, if you have taxes taken out of your RMDs).

If your total estimated tax is at least $1,000, you have to make estimated tax payments. Divide your total estimated tax by four, and pay that amount by each payment due date.

How and When to Make Estimated Tax Payments

The easiest ways to make your estimated federal income tax payments are through the IRS2Go mobile app or online at the IRS website (www.irs.gov/payments). You can pay via direct transfers from your bank account or by credit card, but they do charge a "convenience" fee for card payments. You can also file by regular mail, as long as your payments are postmarked by the due dates (included in the following list).

Check your state's website to find out how to pay your estimated state income taxes, which are usually due on the same dates as the federal payments.

Make sure you submit each quarterly payment by the due date. There are four due dates during the year:

1. April 15
2. June 15
3. September 15
4. January 15 of the following year

When the due date falls on a weekend or a holiday, the official due date will switch to the next business day.

If you're late making an estimated tax payment, do not wait until the next payment date and double up. Send the late payment as soon as possible to minimize (or maybe even avoid) interest charges. The longer you wait to make the payment, the more it will cost you.

AVOIDING TAX PENALTIES

Tax penalties count among the biggest retirement budget busters, but they're easy to avoid if you know about them ahead of time. The most commonly charged penalties include:

- **Late filing penalties:** Avoid these by filing tax returns or extensions by the tax due date.
- **Late payment penalties:** Avoid these by knowing the due dates and sending payments on time.
- **Estimated tax underpayment penalties:** Avoid these by paying at least the "safe harbor" amount.
- **Early distribution penalties:** Avoid these by not taking withdrawals from retirement accounts before age fifty-nine-and-a-half even if you're retired.
- **Excess contribution tax:** Avoid this by not contributing more than the maximum allowable contribution for retirement accounts and health savings accounts.
- **RMD penalty:** Avoid this by taking at least the required minimum distributions from your retirement accounts.

In many cases, if you're hit with a late filing penalty (which can be as much as 25 percent), you'll also have to pay a late payment penalty and possibly an estimated tax underpayment penalty. These tax fees can take a huge chunk out of your savings, so do your best to avoid incurring them.

HOUSING

You've Got to Live Somewhere

One of the biggest questions facing retirees is where they want to live once they've stopped working. No longer tied to an area by commuting time, you can relocate to anywhere in the world. Factor in family ties, cost of living, and comfort zones (city or suburb? warm or cold?) to come up with the optimal choices. Then consider the importance of having a home base: If you plan to do extensive traveling for several years, do you really need to pay a sizeable mortgage or rent? Considering all of these variables before you retire will help you figure out the right housing situation for your family.

WHERE YOU LIVE MATTERS

Cost of living varies widely across the United States and around the world. In some areas, you can live comfortably—even luxuriously—with a relatively small retirement nest egg; in other places, that same level of savings would have you living on the poverty line. It's not just housing costs that will be more affordable; everything from utilities to food will normally be less expensive. Plus, if you move closer to family or toward areas you like to vacation, you'll spend less on travel costs throughout retirement.

In the United States

When it comes to the cost of living, you'll see some wide and wild differences among the fifty states, and even within them. That doesn't mean *every* cost is lower, but it does mean your income will stretch further in lower-cost-of-living areas. And don't forget to look into the state and local taxes. Between property, sales, and income taxes, the potential tax bite can make a substantial difference in your budget. Make sure to factor in all applicable state taxes when you're thinking about making a move to cut expenses.

If you're looking to make a change to a lower cost-of-living area, you'll find no shortage of resources online, from city rankings to comparison calculators. Many also factor in things like healthcare, culture, transportation, and other considerations that can affect daily living. You will discover many resources online that rank states and cities by affordability, including Kiplinger (www.kiplinger.com), *GOBankingRates* (www.gobankingrates.com), and AARP (www.aarp.org).

Outside the United States

A growing number of Americans are retiring outside the United States to take advantage of substantially lower housing costs, lower taxes, lower medical care costs, and a chance at adventure. According to *Forbes* (based on a variety of factors including healthcare, English-speaking prevalence, and cost of living), some of the best countries to retire to include the following:

- Australia
- Chile
- Costa Rica
- Italy
- New Zealand
- Portugal
- Thailand

Keep in mind that buying property outside the US involves several unfamiliar issues, including country-specific document taxes, mortgage availability, and different definitions of property rights. Some countries strictly forbid foreign nationals (which you would be, unless you had dual citizenship) from owning property. In others, foreign nationals can own buildings but not land. Consult with an experienced international attorney and a local (in the target country) real estate attorney to make sure all the legalities are covered.

OWN VERSUS RENT

One of the biggest housing decisions you'll make is whether to own or rent your home, and there's no right answer. Both choices could either help or hurt your financial situation depending on your specific circumstances.

There are some guidelines that do apply universally, though. If you've never owned a home before, retirement is not the time to start. If you can no longer reasonably maintain a home, renting makes more sense. If you're planning to live in your next home for less than five years, don't buy it.

Whichever path you decide to take, keeping costs manageable is the name of the game. For homeowners, that involves paying off the mortgage or refinancing to reduce payments. For renters, it means finding affordable rentals in senior-friendly areas.

Homeowners: Pay Off the Mortgage

One of the best things you can do for yourself before retirement is to pay off your mortgage (but only after you've paid off any higher-interest debt). This is usually the largest *fixed* expense you'll have to shoulder, and it comes with the risk of losing your home if you can't make the monthly payments. Once your home is paid off, you could sell it even in a down market (if you needed to) without worrying about covering the outstanding loan. Finally, paying off your mortgage early can save you an enormous amount of interest; instead of going to the bank, all of that money stays in your nest egg. While you'll still have to pay all of the other costs associated with home ownership, it's much easier without the mortgage—and the consequences of default—hanging over you.

Finding Affordable Rentals

Rents across the US have soared since the housing bubble of 2008–2009 burst as the number of renters hit record highs. Older adults have been the fastest growing group of renters, especially those near retirement. Whether they're looking to downsize space and costs, or get rid of the burden of repairs and maintenance, many senior retirees swap their mortgages for monthly rent. The trick is finding affordable rentals in safe, desirable areas.

GOBankingRates (www.gobankingrates.com) compiled a comprehensive list of the best places (in the US) to retire where you can rent an apartment for no more than $1,000 per month. Their top five choices are the following:

1. El Paso, TX
2. Mesa, AZ
3. Rochester, NY
4. Pensacola, FL
5. Toledo, OH

Along with affordable rent, they looked at features like safety, walkability, and local activities.

Get a Rate Reduction

If you can't pay off your mortgage entirely before you retire and you have a positive relationship with your lender, ask for an interest rate reduction. This helps you pay down your mortgage faster (a larger portion of every payment goes toward principal) and avoids the cost and hassle of refinancing.

DIFFERENT HOUSING OPTIONS

These days, there are many options when it comes to where you'll live during retirement. While many people do choose to stay in their homes or join traditional retirement communities, millions are taking advantage of newer options. Some of these alternatives help reduce housing costs considerably; others may have higher housing costs that are offset by savings in other areas; and some are just straight-up splurges. Whatever your situation is—financially, family-wise, and socially—there's an option that will be perfect for you.

Granny Pods

Granny pods are portable mini-houses that fit into a family member's backyard. They've been around for a few years, and they're being called the "next big thing" in senior living. Granny pods have everything you'd find in a regular house (bathroom, kitchen, bedroom, full utilities, etc.) but in a much smaller space, usually between 300 and 500 square feet. With granny pods, you can be close to family without actually living in the same house, allowing for privacy and independence with aid and companionship just a few feet away. Granny pods range in price from around $37,000 for basic models to more than $125,000 for more luxurious or medically equipped versions.

Senior Cohousing

Communal living is one of the fastest-growing retirement trends, and senior-cohousing communities are cropping up all over the country. In these communities, residents live in completely private rooms but share communal spaces, like yards, kitchens, and entertainment areas. There are frequent community activities to keep residents engaged and interacting, which helps avoid the isolation and loneliness that often strikes retirees, especially after the loss of a significant other. These communities are designed for healthy, active seniors who can contribute to the community in some way. Costs range widely based on the particular community and the amenities provided. You can find a comprehensive listing of cohousing communities at www.cohousing.org.

Luxury Living

Retirees who've spent their lives cutting costs and forgoing wants may want to shift gears and go all-in on luxurious living. Enter upscale senior living communities that offer high-end resort-style living and a care continuum so you never have to move due to health issues. The costs are high, typically involving entrance fees ranging from $100,000 to $1,000,000 plus monthly charges in the thousands, but you do get a lot for that money. Luxury amenities can include the following things:

- Meals prepared by classically trained chefs
- Round-the-clock concierge services

- Full housekeeping services
- Wellness programs
- Spa services
- Wine cellars
- Art and culture courses

On the care side, the continuum runs from fully independent (no care needed) to assisted living to full-time nursing care. Upon death, some communities refund entrance fees to the estate. You can find a luxury senior living community at www.seniorliving.org.

TRANSPORTATION AND TRAVEL

Getting Where You Want to Go

Transportation and travel are two major expense areas for retirees, and both often get overlooked in budget planning. Luckily, you'll usually have more control over these costs than you would for healthcare and housing, which makes them much easier to manage.

TRANSPORTATION

Transportation is one cost that normally drops in retirement, but it still ranks in the top five biggest monthly expenses, especially if you own more than one vehicle. Without the daily commute, you'll save a lot of money on gas driving to work or on monthly transit passes. But this expense won't disappear completely. According to the Bureau of Labor Statistics, the average retiree spends $567 per month on transportation costs, about a third less than their preretirement costs.

Should You Keep the Car(s)?

According to the American Automobile Association (AAA), owning a car costs on average $737 per month; that average accounts for everything from small sedans ($565 per month) to pickup trucks ($851 per month). Costs would be higher with a new car purchase, which typically also comes with ongoing car payments, an additional fixed monthly expense to consider. With two cars to maintain, transportation costs can quickly outpace medical expenses in the retirement budget. That's why many families downsize to a single car in retirement.

Still, if you aren't driving frequently or if you live in a good "walkability" area, going carless can free up a lot of room in your budget. Most areas (though not all) offer at least some form of accessible transportation, and hundreds of communities across the US have access to rideshare services (like Uber and Lyft). And even if alternative transportation methods feel expensive, they still usually add up to much less than the monthly cost of owning a car.

Getting Around Without a Car

If you don't have a car, you won't be stuck at home. There are many ways for retirees to get around, and more options are on the horizon. The most commonly used transportation alternatives include the following:

- Public transportation (usually at reduced senior fares)
- Walking (which comes with substantial health benefits)
- Ride-sharing services, such as Lyft and Uber (which are both expanding their senior-friendly options, including not needing to use a smartphone)

In addition to those common ride-sharing services, seniors have extra options. Veyo (www.veyo.com) contracts with health insurance plans (including Medicare) to offer rides to medical appointments that are not emergencies, with no out-of-pocket costs to the passenger. Many nonprofit organizations and local governments provide low-cost or free shuttle services for seniors (these are prescheduled, like buses).

TRAVEL

A whopping 79 percent of adults expect to travel in retirement (according to the Transamerica Center for Retirement Studies). Most of that is done in the earlier years, while people have the best health and most energy. That's also before their nest eggs are showing the wear and tear of years of withdrawals, which can lead to overspending and future financial issues.

The most important thing to do if you plan to do a lot of traveling: Budget for it. It's common to underestimate travel costs. People focus on the airfare and accommodations but may overlook things like cabs from the airport, tips for housekeeping staff, and gifts for family. Make a thorough spending plan for travel so you won't come up short.

Maximize Travel, Minimize Costs

Retirees have the flexibility to get the most travel for the lowest possible costs without skimping on enjoyment. Here are some ways you can reduce expenses without missing out on the trip of your dreams:

- **Try slow travel:** Keep your travel dates flexible and settle in for the long haul. Book an extended stay in an Airbnb or long-term hotel to minimize lodging costs and really soak up the culture.
- **Travel on off days and during off-season:** Since you're not tied to a work or school schedule, you can go whenever you want. Midweek travel (on Tuesdays and Wednesdays) typically costs less, and so does traveling off-season.
- **Combine trips:** Save on airfare by traveling back-to-back instead of flying home in between. Instead of visiting Paris this year and Rome next year, visit both during the same European vacation.

- **Consider alternative destinations:** Some parts of the world are just more expensive to visit than others. Swap mediocre accommodations in Paris for a luxury stay in Thailand or Costa Rica.
- **Use a travel rewards card wisely:** When used properly, travel rewards cards offer a multitude of benefits (like travel insurance) plus substantial savings on future travel. Only use this strategy if you can (and will) pay the bill in full every month.

Plan for Medical Care

If you'll be doing a lot of traveling, especially outside the US, make sure to plan ahead for medical care. People with chronic health conditions or on medication need to make sure they find appropriate care and resources. Also, Medicare doesn't cover medical expenses outside the country (with some exceptions for inpatient care in Canada or Mexico). While some Medicare Advantage plans do offer overseas coverage, most don't, so check your policy carefully before you set off on your adventure. To bridge any coverage gaps, think about getting travel medical insurance to cover you no matter where you are.

Cruise Coverage

If you need medical care while on a cruise ship, Medicare *might* pick up the cost, as long as it meets two conditions. First, the doctor is allowed by law to provide medical services on the ship. Second, the ship can't be more than six hours away from a US port when you receive the services.

CARING FOR FAMILY

We're All in This Together

Elderly parents are running out of money. Adult children can't find sufficient work or affordable housing. Grandchildren need a caretaker and no one else is around.

All three of these scenarios are becoming increasingly common, and each can take a significant toll on your financial security. The only way to keep the family—and yourself—afloat is through careful planning and clear expectations.

AGING PARENTS

As people are living longer than ever before, it's not unusual for retirement savings to get used up. In fact, according to www.care .com, around 25 percent of Americans help support their parents. While Medicaid may kick in to cover some healthcare expenses, it doesn't cover everything else, like rent and food. Without pensions to rely on and no nest egg to turn to, millions of elderly adults turn to their children, now in retirement themselves, for help. This can take a huge emotional and financial toll, and it requires a lot of thought and planning to make sure you don't wind up in the same situation.

Work Out a Plan

Though time may be short, this situation calls for an intensive family financial planning session that includes your siblings (and it often helps to work with a neutral professional). You'll need to compare the costs (including emotional costs) of keeping your parents in their home, moving them into your home, or helping them downsize into a more affordable place. If they require care, look into assisted living or nursing home facilities (even if you don't expect them to go there) to work out care costs. Their only financial contribution may be Social Security, and that needs to factor into the overall family budget now.

Use Every Available Resource

There are a lot of social safety nets out there, but you have to seek them out. Here are some resources to get you started:

- The US Department of Housing and Urban Development (www.hud.gov) offers a wealth of housing-related resources, including federal housing assistance, help paying utility bills, and a guide to available state resources (such as property tax relief programs).
- The National Association of Area Agencies on Aging (www.n4a.org) serves as a central source for local organizations throughout the country that help older adults age in place by providing resources for food, housing, healthcare, and other programs.
- The Administration for Community Living (www.acl.gov) provides resources and information to help senior citizens remain in their communities and offers assistance to their caregivers.
- SeniorLiving.org (www.seniorliving.org) has a comprehensive guide to government aid for seniors, covering areas such as housing, food, health, and employment.

ADULT CHILDREN

When it comes to helping their children financially, the vast majority of parents are willing to do so...even at their own expense. That includes parents who are nearing or in retirement, which can leave them short on financial security.

Helping your children is the most natural thing, but there are ways to help your children without shortchanging yourself. Setting appropriate limits, guiding them back toward an independent path, and keeping an eye on your financial picture all figure in to keeping the overall family finances in better shape.

If you want to help your adult children financially, do it strategically to minimize the drag on your long-term financial security. Talk with your financial advisor about the best ways to *temporarily* support your children until they get back on their feet. Involve your children in this conversation after you have a plan in place. The strategies will look different depending on whether you're still working or have already retired, but these are guidelines that work for both:

- Don't take on debt to provide support for your children.
- Avoid pulling money from retirement accounts (before you've retired) whenever possible.
- If you have to take money from retirement accounts, be prepared to pay taxes and possibly tax penalties.
- Set both a dollar limit and a time limit for the assistance.
- Help your children develop realistic emergency budgets for this situation.

By following these basic guidelines, you'll be more likely to avoid dire financial consequences from the help you extend to your children.

GRANDCHILDREN

A surprising number of households skip a generation, comprising grandparents and grandchildren—more than 2.5 million, according to a US Census Bureau estimate. This type of living arrangement can throw a monkey wrench into the best-laid retirement plans. Now, instead of primarily focusing on lowering your cost of living, you'll have to consider things like school districts and braces. That will make it much harder to stretch your retirement savings, but not impossible with some careful planning. It really pays to work with a financial advisor here, especially if you will be the permanent or long-term care provider for your grandchildren.

Finding Resources

There are tons of resources available for "grandfamily" households, offering all kinds of assistance, from financial to childcare to legal issues (like registering children for school). Grandfamilies .org (www.grandfamilies.org) makes a great starting point, listing federal and local resources in pretty much every category you can imagine. The AARP website (www.aarp.org) also contains a wealth of information and discussion groups to help you navigate raising your grandchildren.

Take Every Possible Tax Credit

If you are supporting a dependent child, you may be eligible for some beneficial tax credits and deductions. The IRS has seven requirements you have to meet (mostly about child eligibility), but if you are financially supporting and caring for a grandchild under age seventeen in your home, you'll almost certainly qualify. It's a good idea to work with a tax professional, especially the first year you're filing as the caretaker, to make sure you're accounting for every reduction possible.

The Child Tax Credit is a partially refundable credit (meaning you may get more money back than you paid in taxes). The maximum credit is $2,000 per qualifying child, with a refundable portion of up to $1,400 each. If you pay for childcare for a grandchild under age thirteen, you may also be able to take the Dependent Care Credit. The maximum possible credit is $1,050 for one child or $2,100 for two or more children.

The Earned Income Tax Credit

If you're working (in any capacity) and earning money, you may qualify for the earned income tax credit (EITC). This credit is also refundable. Visit the IRS website at www.irs.gov for details and find out whether your situation qualifies. The IRS is very strict about this credit in particular, but if you are eligible for it, definitely take it.

Chapter 6

Navigating Social Security and Medicare

Figuring out Social Security and Medicare is much trickier than most people realize. The choices you make can have big effects on your monthly income and expenses that last through your whole retirement. On the Social Security side, the big issue is deciding when to start taking benefits. With Medicare, there are even more issues to wade through, and those can change every year, sometimes even within a single year. Understanding how both programs work and knowing the deadlines in play *before* you have to make those choices will make navigating Social Security and Medicare much easier to deal with.

HOW SOCIAL SECURITY RETIREMENT BENEFITS WORK

Collecting the Check

Collecting Social Security retirement benefits sounds simple, but it's more complicated than just signing up. To get the most out of Social Security, you'll need to do some careful planning and make some strategic decisions. Knowing how your benefits are calculated and what you can do to maximize them will help you make the best decisions for your situation.

What You Pay In

If you earn income—meaning if you work for yourself or for an employer—you are paying into Social Security. All workers pay 6.2 percent of their salaries or wages (up to a set annual limit) toward Social Security every year. Employers pay an additional 6.2 percent of each worker's earnings. Self-employed people pay both parts, sending 12.4 percent of their earnings to Social Security.

YOUR FULL RETIREMENT BENEFITS

Your full retirement benefits through Social Security are calculated based on the money you earned over your lifetime. The goal is to help replace the income you've lost by retiring so you can cover your essential expenses. The two main factors here are the number of years you've worked and how much you've earned each year. If your employment history spans less than thirty-five years, your full retirement benefits could be lower than someone who's worked for that long, even if you had higher earnings in those years (zero earnings years lower your average).

The big takeaway here is this: The more money you paid in, the more money you'll get out.

Benefit Math

The SSA (Social Security Administration) takes your actual historical Social Security earnings and "indexes" them (which really just means "adjusts" them) to account for the general increase in average wages over time. (For example, a salary earned in 1990 would be adjusted to "catch up" to the current equivalent salary level.) Then, they figure out your average indexed monthly earnings (AIME) based on the thirty-five years that you earned the most money. Using a complicated formula, they convert your AIME into your primary insurance amount (PIA), also known as your full retirement benefits.

Keep in mind that this only includes earnings that you paid Social Security taxes on, and those taxes come with an earnings cap ($132,900 for 2019). If you earned more than the cap in any year, only the amount up to the cap counts toward your future retirement benefits.

Social Security Credits

In addition to the money you earned, the SSA also looks at your work credits. To get Social Security retirement benefits, you need to earn at least 40 credits throughout your life. Every year, you have the opportunity to earn 4 credits. So, you'd have to work a total of ten years (but not necessarily in a row) to qualify for benefits.

Credits are tied to the money you earn, which includes salary, wages, and self-employment income (basically, any income you had to pay Social Security taxes on). Since credits are based on money and not time, you can earn all 4 credits for a year without actually working during the entire year. The dollar value of credits can change over time. In 2019, you get a credit for every $1,360 earned; earning $5,440 would net you all 4 credits for the year.

For Spouses

Social Security works differently for couples. If both you and your spouse earned enough credits, you'll both qualify for Social Security retirement benefits. But if one of you didn't work, or didn't earn nearly as much as the other and qualifies for less than half the benefits of the high earner, the lower earning spouse will get a benefit bump-up to half of the higher earner's benefits. For example, if one spouse got $2,000 per month and the other got a $900 monthly benefit, the $900 would increase to $1,000 (half of $2,000).

Should one spouse die, the other is entitled to survivor benefits if they are at least sixty years old or have a common child under age sixteen. The surviving spouse only receives 100 percent of their spouse's benefits if they have reached their full retirement age (FRA). Otherwise, the benefits are reduced. If the surviving spouse is already collecting Social Security, they'll continue to get whichever benefits are bigger.

CREATE A "*MY* SOCIAL SECURITY" ACCOUNT

"*My* Social Security" is a secure online portal where you can review and manage your Social Security benefits. Once you open your account, you can look over your earnings history to make sure it's accurate, and get an idea of your future benefits based on your planned retirement age. You can also request replacement documents (if you've lost your Social Security card, for example).

Only you can set up your "*my* Social Security" account. Even if you give someone else permission (even in writing) to do it for you, they can't. That works both ways: You also cannot set up an account for someone else. Applying for an account for someone else can result in potentially steep civil and criminal penalties.

How to Create the Account

Creating your account takes about ten to fifteen minutes online. To set up your "*my* Social Security" account, head over to the Social Security website at www.ssa.gov. You'll need to enter your name as it appears on your Social Security card, a valid email account, a US mailing address, and your Social Security number to get started. Next, you'll see a page of identity verification questions, asking for the following information:

- Your monthly mortgage payment
- Your mortgage provider
- Previous names
- Previous addresses
- Old phone numbers

Once you've cleared that hurdle, the system will send a verification code to you by text or email, and then let you through to your new "*my* Social Security" account.

Verify Your Earnings Record

As soon as you create your account, review your earnings record to make sure it's correct. Your Social Security retirement benefits are based on your past earnings, and mistakes here can make a giant difference in your retirement income. Be aware that this only includes your Social Security earnings, which are subject to an annual cap; if you earned more than that, it won't show up on your statement. If you spot a mistake, call Social Security at 1-800-772-1213 to report it.

Every year, around three months before your birthday, the SSA will email you a reminder to check your Social Security Statement. That email won't contain or ask for any personal information; if you get an email that does, don't click on anything and send it to your spam folder.

WHEN SHOULD I START TAKING SOCIAL SECURITY?

Is Now Too Soon?

One of the biggest questions facing retirees is when to start taking Social Security. You can start taking benefits any time between ages sixty-two and seventy, but when you start can make an enormous difference in your monthly payments.

Age is not the only factor to consider when you're making this choice, though. Your monthly income and expenses, marital status, and estimated life expectancy will all come into play. The decision starts with knowing your full retirement benefits and your full retirement age.

KNOW YOUR FULL RETIREMENT AGE

Full retirement age, or FRA, is the age you can start taking *full* retirement benefits. Sounds simple, but it's not quite as straightforward as it seems. Your FRA is based on the year you were born, and your actual benefits depend on whether you begin taking them before, at, or after your FRA. According to the SSA, here's how the FRAs fall out:

- Age sixty-six and six months for people born in 1957
- Age sixty-six and eight months for people born in 1958
- Age sixty-six and ten months for people born in 1959
- Age sixty-seven for people born in 1960 and later

Chances are, FRAs will increase in the near future. Whatever happens, be aware of your FRA before you apply for benefits.

Reduced Benefits for "Early" Retirees

You can start collecting Social Security retirement benefits as soon as you turn age sixty-two—and many people mistakenly believe that's the age they're supposed to start taking Social Security. However, if you start taking benefits before you hit your FRA, you'll receive smaller monthly payments for the rest of your life. For example, by starting at age sixty-two, you'll receive only 75 percent of your full retirement benefit each month. The amount is reduced because you'll be getting those payments for a longer period of time, which means you may actually get more money in total over your lifetime.

Better Benefits after FRA

Once you reach your FRA, you'll get your full retirement benefits. But if you wait a little longer, your monthly payment will be increased. The longer you wait, the more you get. In fact, starting at age seventy results in a payment that's about 77 percent more money than you'd get starting at age sixty-two.

The table below shows how the monthly payment would change for someone born in 1970 with a PIA (primary insurance amount) of $1,500 based on the age they start taking benefits.

AGE	MONTHLY BENEFIT AMOUNT
62	$1,050
63	$1,125
64	$1,200
65	$1,300

AGE	MONTHLY BENEFIT AMOUNT
66	$1,400
67	$1,500
68	$1,620
69	$1,740
70	$1,860

You can see how waiting as long as you can maximizes your monthly benefits.

A LOOK AT THE OTHER FACTORS

In addition to your age, you need to consider some other key factors before deciding when to apply for benefits. Depending on your unique circumstances, it may make sense to get benefits as early as possible or to delay as long as possible. There's no "right time" that works for everyone (no matter what you read online). The three important considerations other than your FRA are budget issues, marital status, and expected longevity. You have to factor all of these into your Social Security decision to make the best choice for your financial future.

Cover Your Budget

If you're having a hard time making ends meet, applying for Social Security benefits as early as possible may seem like the best option. But consider this: By locking into reduced benefits now, you're also locking into smaller cost of living increases (which are calculated as a percentage of your benefits). Since prices seem to only go up, that can put a huge dent in your future purchasing power, when it will be even harder to make up the income in other ways. On top of that, if you live into your eighties or nineties (which is becoming the norm), taking early Social Security before your FRA could cost you more than $100,000 in lifetime benefits.

If you can find a way to boost your income without collecting Social Security before you hit your FRA, you'll be offering your future self a better chance of keeping even inflation-increased expenses covered.

If You're Married, Decide As a Couple

The decision about when to apply for Social Security is fairly straightforward for single people. A lot of married people work out their timing based on single-people factors, but it can be much more lucrative to coordinate and plan this out as a couple.

Also, married couples have more to consider because of the way survivor benefits work (which was covered earlier in this chapter). When one spouse dies, the surviving spouse can continue to receive whichever benefit is larger. By planning ahead as a couple, you'll help ensure that the surviving spouse gets maximum benefits.

Longevity

No one likes to think about life expectancy, but it plays a supersized role in your retirement planning—and that includes your decision about when to apply for Social Security benefits. Of course, it's impossible to predict your longevity with certainty, but you can make an educated estimate. Take an honest look at your health, lifestyle, and family history. Then, plug some basic information into a life expectancy calculator (you can find one online at www.bankrate .com or on most life insurance company websites).

For people with "standard" life expectancy (around eighty years), applying right at the FRA tends to offer the biggest lifetime benefits (even though you could get a higher monthly benefit by delaying). If your life expectancy is less than average, taking early benefits makes more sense. With a longer-than-average life expectancy, delaying benefits for as long as possible gives you the biggest monthly paycheck for the longest time.

Average Life Expectancy

According to the CDC (the Centers for Disease Control and Prevention), the overall average life expectancy for American adults is 78.6 years. When you break it out by gender, men live an average of 76.1 years, while women live an average of 81.1 years.

YOU CAN CHANGE YOUR MIND

If you've applied for Social Security and then realize you don't need it, you may be able to "unapply." There are two different processes to halt benefits, and which one you'll use depends on whether or not you've reached your full retirement age.

Before Full Retirement Age

To withdraw your claim after receiving Social Security retirement benefits before reaching your full retirement age (FRA), you need to meet two conditions: It has to be within twelve months of when you filed for benefits, and you cannot have withdrawn your claim before (it's a one-shot deal). If you meet both criteria, you'll have to fill out Form SSA-521 and mail (or bring) it to your local Social Security office. You can find the form and locate your Social Security office on the SSA website at www.ssa.gov. Look for the "If You Change Your Mind" page.

When your withdrawal gets approved, payments to you and any family members getting benefits from that claim (such as spousal benefits) will stop. You will also have to repay the benefits you and your family have already received. The SSA will tell you how much you owe them and how to pay it. Basically, you're buying back your right to collect benefits at a later date, which will almost always be larger. Be aware that you may face some tax issues, so it's a good idea to get your CPA involved before you submit the withdrawal form.

If you change your mind about withdrawing your claim, you have sixty days to do so once your withdrawal has been approved.

After Full Retirement Age

Once you've reached your FRA, you can suspend your Social Security retirement benefits at any time until you reach age seventy (the maximum age to start collecting benefits). To temporarily suspend your benefits, you can call the SSA (1-800-772-1213) or mail them a written request (no special form for this). Since Social Security retirement benefits are paid a month behind, you'll still get one month's benefit payment after you suspend them (so if you suspend in March, you'll still get March's payment in April).

You can restart your benefits at any time you want. Simply notify Social Security verbally or in writing, and your benefits will start back up. Benefits will kick in automatically when you turn age seventy if you haven't already resumed them. You can find the appropriate phone number or mailing address on the Social Security website at www.ssa.gov.

HOW TO APPLY FOR SOCIAL SECURITY

Sign Me Up

When you're ready to start receiving Social Security benefits, you have to apply with the Social Security Administration (SSA). You'll have a choice between applying online, over the phone, or in person at your local Social Security office. Whichever way you go, you'll need to supply some basic information and may have to show them proof of eligibility.

IT'S EASY TO APPLY ONLINE

The SSA makes it very easy to apply for benefits online through their website www.ssa.gov. The application is easy to deal with, and it typically takes less than thirty minutes to fill out. Before you apply for benefits, you'll need to have a *my* Social Security" account set up. You'll also want to have some basic information on hand, including the following:

- Your birthdate and Social Security number
- Your marriage date(s)
- Proof of citizenship
- Bank account and routing number (for direct deposit)
- Military service history
- Work history

Once you submit the application, you're done. If the agency has any questions or needs more information from you (which sometimes happens), they'll get in touch with you by phone or snail mail.

Three Simple Steps to Apply

Once you're ready to apply, go to the SSA website at www.ssa .gov and click on "Retirement." Then, all it takes is three easy steps to apply for Social Security benefits.

1. Click on the "Apply for Retirement Benefits" button, then sign in to your "*my* Social Security" account. The site will take you through a bunch of screens with questions about you and your work.
2. Fill out the application. You can do the whole thing in one session or start now and finish later.
3. Click on "Submit Now" to send the application electronically.

Once you're done, you'll get a receipt that you can print or save for your records. You'll be able to check the application status when it's one month until you'll start collecting benefits.

IF YOU CAN'T APPLY ONLINE

Whether you don't have secure Internet access or are not eligible to apply online, you can sign up for Social Security in person by visiting the local office. Agency employees there will verify your supporting documents and help you fill out the necessary paperwork.

You cannot file your application online for Social Security benefits if one of these conditions applies to you:

- You've applied for retirement benefits before and suspended them, but now need them reinstated.
- You're not at least sixty-one years and eight months old.
- It's more than four months in advance of when you want to start receiving benefits.

One common cause for the last two reasons: People who will be traveling abroad may need to apply for benefits before setting off on their journeys.

While you don't need an appointment to apply for benefits, making one helps reduce waiting times. To make an appointment, call Social Security at 1-800-772-1213 or contact your local Social Security office directly. You can find your local office using the Social Security Office Locator tool at www.ssa.gov.

Track the Status

Even if you apply for Social Security in person, you can still track your application status online through your "*my* Social Security" account. If you don't have Internet access (or don't want to check online), you can call the main Social Security number (1-800-772-1213) or the local office where you completed your application.

OTHER INCOME AFFECTS YOUR BENEFITS

Why Am I Getting Less?!

Many retirees find that Social Security alone isn't enough to keep the lights on. They often wind up going back to work to make up the difference, only to find their Social Security retirement benefits reduced or taxed. Before you venture back into the job market, figure out how much you'll need to earn to make up for any reduction in benefits or extra taxes you'll have to pay.

EARNED INCOME AFFECTS THE BENEFIT AMOUNT

A lot of people continue to work or go back to work while they collect Social Security retirement benefits. That can affect the amount of monthly benefits they receive. If they earn more than the SSA limit, their benefits will get reduced. On the flip side, it may also serve to increase their benefits if they earn more than they did in any one of the thirty-five years used to calculate the original full retirement benefit.

Age Matters

Earned income affects your benefits differently based on how old you are. If you start taking benefits before your FRA, the annual earnings threshold is pretty low (just $17,640 in 2019). Once you make more money than that, the SSA deducts $1 from your benefit for every $2 that you earn above the limit. For example, if you earned $5,000 over the limit, your annual benefits would be reduced by $2,500 (or around $208 per month).

In the year before you reach your FRA, that formula changes. You can earn more (up to $46,920 in 2019) and your benefits will be reduced by less—the SSA deducts $1 for every $3 you earn over the limit, but only until the month you reach your FRA. After you have reached your full retirement age, you can earn as much as you want and your benefits won't be reduced at all.

You Have to Tell Them

The SSA doesn't track your earnings while you're receiving benefits. They don't know if your benefits should be reduced because you made more than the earnings limit. It's your responsibility to notify them if you're going to earn enough to cross that earnings threshold.

If you don't tell them, they will find out when you file your tax return. If you received excess benefits because of your earnings, you could be hit with fines. You'll also either need to pay back the excess amount or get reduced benefits going forward.

Special Payments Won't Affect It

The SSA has a whole list of "special payments" that seem like earned income, but they disregard these when it comes to your monthly benefit. These mainly involve pay that was earned in the past but received in the present, after you stopped working. Examples of special payments include the following:

- Severance pay
- Bonuses
- Unused vacation or sick days

- Back pay
- Deferred compensation (like stock options)
- Commissions

The SSA can't tell the different between regular earned income and special payments, so you need to let them know if you've received any—especially if those payments put you over the income limit for the year.

What Counts Toward the Earnings Test?

The SSA only considers income from work activity to be earned income. That includes wages, salaries, commissions, and self-employment income. Income from other sources (such as rental properties, pensions, and investment earnings) doesn't come into play here.

MOST INCOME AFFECTS TAXES

Many people mistakenly believe that Social Security retirement benefits aren't taxable. That's not quite true; depending on your overall income level, you may have to pay taxes on your Social Security income. When it comes to taxation of these benefits (as opposed to reduction of benefits), almost everything counts as income. However, no matter how much income you have, you won't be taxed on more than 85 percent of your Social Security income.

Under the IRS rules, you'll owe taxes on at least a portion of your Social Security retirement benefits if "combined income" exceeds their limits. Combined income here means your total adjusted gross income (AGI) (your total taxable income before standard or itemized deductions), plus any nontaxable interest you earned (such as that earned on municipal bonds) plus half of the Social Security benefits you received.

The income limits here are lower than most people think, especially when you consider that the average annual Social Security retirement benefits come to more than $17,000. According to the IRS (for 2019), your benefits will be partially taxable if:

- You file as single with combined income of at least $25,000.
- You file as married-joint with combined income of at least $32,000.
- You file as married-separate (almost always regardless of income).

If you think you're going to owe taxes on your Social Security benefits, you can either add more money to your estimated tax payments or have federal (but not state) income taxes withheld from your benefit checks. If you go the withholding route, you can have either 7 percent, 10 percent, 12 percent, or 22 percent of your benefits withheld; you can't request specific dollar amounts or other percentages. You'll need to fill out Form W-4 (available on the IRS website, www.irs.gov) and mail or bring it to your local Social Security office.

UNDERSTAND THE DIFFERENT PARTS OF MEDICARE

The ABCDs of Medicare

Medicare supplies primary insurance coverage to Americans older than age sixty-five. It seems like it should be simple to navigate, but it's not. Medicare is extremely complicated, with four different parts and a lot of shifting deadlines. Most people focus on what the various parts of Medicare cover, but what they *don't* cover is even more important. Having a good understanding of that will help you choose the Medicare plans and (possibly) supplement insurance plans that are right for you.

MEDICARE PART A

Medicare Part A acts as hospital insurance, and it's free for most Americans. As long as you or your spouse has paid in to the program for at least forty quarters, you won't have to pay a premium for this coverage. Basically, if you qualify for Social Security retirement benefits, you will also automatically qualify for Part A. If you don't qualify for free Part A, you may still be able to get the coverage by paying a monthly premium.

Part A covers things like inpatient stays, hospice care, some home healthcare, and skilled nursing facilities (such as stroke rehabilitation centers, for example). All of these services are subject to annual copays and deductibles. Part A doesn't cover any individual doctor bills racked up during inpatient stays; those may be covered by Part B. You can visit www.medicare.gov to find out current out-of-pocket costs and more detailed coverage information.

Keep in mind that Medicare only covers a portion of the cost for nursing facilities, and only if it immediately follows a minimum three-day inpatient hospital stay. That means Medicare does not cover long-term care under any other circumstance, leaving most people on the hook to pay for their own long-term care. (You can find information on long-term care coverage in Chapter 5.)

Sign up for Part A as soon as you're eligible, whether or not you're covered by an employer-sponsored plan. Since the coverage is free (for most people), there's no downside to enrolling.

What If My Doctor Doesn't Take Medicare

Many doctors don't accept Medicare, but that doesn't mean you can't still go to them. In most cases, you'll have to pay the bill up front, then submit a claim to Medicare; you won't get the full amount back, but they will cover at least a portion. If that doesn't fit with your budget, you can find a new doctor that does accept Medicare using the Physician Compare directory on their website at www.medicare.gov.

MEDICARE PART B

Part B is similar to regular medical insurance. It covers things like "medically necessary" doctor visits, most lab tests, and some preventive healthcare services (like bone density tests, cancer screening, and an annual checkup).

You have to pay a monthly premium for this coverage. And you may also have to shell out money for copays and deductibles, sometimes up to 20 percent of the cost, based on the specific services you use.

While Part B offers at least partial coverage for many healthcare services, there's a lot that it doesn't cover, which takes many people by surprise. By knowing ahead of time what Part B does and does not cover, and which services will be subject to copays and deductibles, you'll be better able to budget for your healthcare costs.

Where Copays and Deductibles Kick In

While you probably won't have to pay anything for preventive care doctor visits and screening tests, most other types of care come with a price tag in the forms of copays and deductibles. Part B deductibles are pretty low (starting at around $135, then possibly increasing based on your income). Copays are usually 20 percent of the "approved Medicare cost" for the services you get.

Here are just a few of the services that are only partially covered by Medicare Part B:

- Outpatient chemotherapy
- Diabetes supplies
- Wheelchairs and walkers
- Oxygen
- Dialysis
- Physical therapy
- Diagnostic tests (like MRIs or CT scans)

If you have a chronic health condition or use a lot of healthcare services, you may benefit from adding Part C coverage to your Medicare plan.

What Part B Does *Not* Cover

Most people are unpleasantly surprised when they find out what Medicare Part B does not cover, which includes the following items:

- Prescription medications
- Dental care
- Eye exams
- Acupuncture
- Corrective lenses (glasses or contacts)
- Hearing aids
- Long-term care

Part B also does not cover most types of natural or alternative medical services (except chiropractors, which it does cover).

MEDICARE PART C

Medicare Part C is also known as the Medicare Advantage plan. The government does not provide this coverage; rather, it's provided by private health insurers. For that reason, plan premiums, benefits, copays, and deductibles vary widely.

These plans are more like the health coverage you're used to, standard health maintenance organization (HMO) or preferred provider organization (PPO) plans. They cover many more services than original Medicare, and often (but *not* always) charge smaller copays and deductibles. The flip side: They charge higher premiums. However, for many people, the higher premium will be more than offset by the expanded coverage. When you join one of these plans, they provide hospital and medical coverage.

Different Types of Medicare Part C Plans

There are several different types of Medicare Part C plans to choose from. Which will work best for you depends on how particular you are about the doctors you see, your budget, and your overall healthcare usage. The types of Part C plans include the following:

- HMOs (health maintenance organizations), which cover only in-network doctors, hospitals, labs, and pharmacies (unless there's an emergency). You'll usually need a referral from your primary care doctor to see any other doctor.
- PPOs (preferred provider organizations), which offer more coverage for in-network providers and less coverage (they pay less) for out-of-network providers; however, you can generally go to any doctor you want.
- SNPs (special needs plans), which provide more focused coverage, and work best for people with chronic health conditions or people living in skilled nursing facilities.

Once you know which type of plan best fits your situation, you can search for individual plans under that category within Medicare's Plan Finder.

Know the Costs

Your out-of-pocket costs can vary widely based on the plan you choose. When you're weighing the options, make sure to include every cost of the plan, from premiums to copays to deductibles. Remember, these are private plans, and they decide how much they'll reimburse for the services you use.

Each fall, you'll get two documents from your plan. The first one is called Evidence of Coverage (EOC), and includes details of what the plan will cover and how much you will pay (among other things). Also, they have to inform you in writing with an Annual Notice of Change (ANOC) of anything that will be different from the prior coverage year. Part C plans are only allowed to change their pricing and coverage (which services or doctors they will cover) once a year.

5-Star Plans

Every year, Medicare rates and ranks all of the Part C and D plans based on user satisfaction, quality of care, and performance. Whenever possible, choose 5-star plans because these have the best ratings. They're easy to spot because they're all marked with a little gold star icon in Medicare's Plan Finder.

MEDICARE PART D

Part D is all about prescription drug coverage; this is one of the most complicated parts of Medicare. There are many Part D plans, and they each cover only a specific list of prescription drugs. Those lists can change from year to year, and even within a plan year (meaning a medication you take could be covered at the beginning of the year, then dropped by the plan during the year, so you're forced to pay out-of-pocket).

Know Your Drugs

Before you choose a Part D plan, make a list of all the prescription medications you take and their dosages. Some plans cover drugs only at specific dosages, so make sure to check. Your copays will depend on the specific drugs you take and the pharmacies you use (more on that in just a second).

You may also need to get special advance authorization for more expensive prescriptions. Your doctor may have to explain why the particular drug is medically necessary before the Part D plan will agree to cover it. The plan might *require* you to try a less costly drug first, and only allow the medication your doctor recommends if it doesn't work.

Preferred Pharmacies

The latest trend in Medicare Part D plans is working with preferred pharmacies. These policies come with lower premiums, which can offset rising medical costs. You can minimize your copays by using only the preferred pharmacies, whether they're brick-and-mortar stores or mail-order pharmacies. Be aware that your copays will almost certainly be higher if you choose a different pharmacy—so make sure the preferred pharmacy for the plan is easy for you to use.

HOW AND WHEN TO APPLY FOR MEDICARE

Get Your Timing Right

If you're coming up on your sixty-fifth birthday, it's time to know the ins and outs of Medicare enrollment, especially when it comes to sign-up dates. Medicare has many different deadlines for both original enrollment and any plan changes you want to make. The deadlines are weird, and missing them could result in higher "penalty" premiums for the rest of your life.

Before you sign up, take the time to decide which plans you want to enroll in. Most people start with Parts A and B ("original" Medicare), then eventually add in Parts C and D.

HOW TO ENROLL IN MEDICARE

If you start collecting Social Security retirement benefits at least four months before you turn sixty-five, you'll automatically be enrolled in Medicare Parts A and B. How will you know if you're enrolled? You'll receive a red, white, and blue Medicare card three months before your birthday.

In every other circumstance, you have to proactively apply for Medicare benefits through the SSA. You can apply for Parts A and B online at www.ssa.gov, call the SSA at 1-800-772-1213, or visit your local Social Security office.

You can enroll in Parts C (Medicare Advantage) and D (prescription drug coverage) during your original enrollment period, or during one of the special enrollment periods (more on timing in the next section). Because private insurers run these plans, the sign up process is different than it is for original Medicare.

Scam Alert: They Won't Call You

Medicare Advantage plans will never call you unless you have initiated the call (like when they're calling you back with information you requested). They are not allowed to call you in any other circumstance. And they will never ask for personal financial information (like bank account numbers) over the phone. If you get a cold call from a Medicare Advantage plan, hang up—it's a scam.

Before you can enroll in a Medicare Advantage plan or Part D coverage, you have to choose the plans you want. You can find a full listing of plans available in your area by using Medicare's Plan Finder at www.medicare.gov. Once you've chosen a plan, you have to go to that plan's website to apply. Some Medicare Advantage plans include drug coverage. If the one you select does not cover the prescription drugs you're currently taking, you'll want to sign up for separate Part D (prescription drug) coverage. To apply for Parts C and D, you'll need to know your original Medicare enrollment date and your Medicare ID number, both of which are on your Medicare card.

ORIGINAL ENROLLMENT

You can enroll in Medicare right before you reach age sixty-five. Your initial enrollment period starts three months before your birthday month and continues for three months after it, for a total seven-month window. Whenever you sign up (within the window), your benefits will kick in on the first day of your birthday month. So, if you sign up after your birthday, you'll be covered retroactively.

If you miss the window, you'll almost certainly be hit with a penalty. Your Part B premiums could increase by 10 percent for each twelve-month period you could have had Part B, but didn't sign up. Those premium hikes will stick with you for as long as you have Medicare Part B. Once you've missed your window, you'll have to wait until the next Part B general enrollment period. That runs from January 1 to March 31 each year to sign up for coverage beginning the following July 1. So, missing the sign-up window could leave you stuck in a costly coverage gap.

If you don't want Part B coverage because you're still working and are covered by an employer health insurance plan, special rules apply as long as your employer has at least twenty employees. You can delay Part B enrollment and sidestep the penalty premiums as long as you do sign up within eight months of losing your employer coverage. That eight-month window applies even if you decide to continue your employer coverage through COBRA. Visit www.medicare.gov for more information about this exception.

Once you're enrolled in original Medicare, you'll have two months to enroll in a Part C (Medicare Advantage) plan and Part D (prescription drug) coverage.

Stop Contributing to Your HSA *Before* You Enroll

Once you've enrolled in Medicare, you cannot contribute to an HSA (health savings account) anymore. Since Medicare Part A may cover you for up to six months *retroactively*, stop making HSA contributions at least six months before you plan to apply.

CHANGING YOUR COVERAGE

Once you're enrolled in Medicare, you'll have an opportunity every year to add, drop, or make changes to your coverage under Parts C and D. There are two distinct open enrollment periods every year, and you can do different things during each one.

Open Enrollment, Part I

The first open enrollment period runs from October 15 through December 7 of every year. During that period, you are allowed to:

- Add or drop a Part C (Medicare Advantage) plan
- Switch from one Part C plan to another
- Switch from a Part C plan that doesn't cover prescriptions to one that does (or vice versa)
- Add or drop Part D (prescription drug) coverage
- Switch from one Part D plan to another

Any changes you make during this enrollment period take effect on January 1.

Open Enrollment, Part II

The second open enrollment period, which runs from January 1 through March 31 of every year, is more limited. You can make one (and only one) change:

- Switch from one Part C plan to another
- Drop your Part C plan entirely (so you'd be covered by Part B for medical) and add a Part D plan

During this period, you *cannot* initiate Part C coverage, join a Part D plan (if you were already covered only by original Medicare), or switch Part D plans. Any changes you do make during this period kick in on the first of the next month after you make the change.

SPECIAL ENROLLMENT PERIOD

Depending on your situation, you may be able to sign up for Medicare during a Special Enrollment Period (SEP). If you participate in a group health plan through your (or your spouse's) employer and delayed your original enrollment, you can sign up for Medicare Parts A and B at any time while you're still covered under that plan. You also qualify for an eight-month SEP that begins when either your employment or your employer coverage ends. (Remember, COBRA coverage does not count here; that's considered individual and NOT group coverage.)

There are also some circumstances that trigger SEPs for Part C and D changes. Examples include the following:

- You move outside your plan's service area.
- You move inside your plan's service area, and new plan options are available based on your new address.
- Medicare drops your plan.
- You move into or out of a skilled nursing facility.

You can find a full listing of events that trigger SEPs on the Medicare website at www.medicare.gov.

REVIEW YOUR MEDICARE PLANS EVERY YEAR

Not the Same As Last Time

When it comes to your medical expenses, there are a lot of moving parts. On the Medicare side, if you're enrolled in Part C or Part D plans, you face a lot of potential changes. On the personal side, your healthcare needs can change dramatically from year to year. That's why it's crucial to take a fresh look at your Medicare plans every year before the open enrollment periods end.

EVALUATE YOUR PART C PLAN

People are often reluctant to make changes to their healthcare coverage, but when your coverage comes from a Medicare Advantage (Part C) plan, it's often the smartest move both medically and financially. Even if you had a great experience with the plan during the prior year, the plan itself may have undergone changes. In fact, it's extremely rare for there to be no changes at all—and you don't want to be stuck with a plan that no longer meets your healthcare needs.

On top of that, your plan may no longer be available next year. Some plans withdraw from certain service areas while others don't renew their Medicare contracts.

Read the ANOC
Every September, you'll receive an ANOC (Annual Notice of Changes) for your Medicare Advantage plan, well in advance of the

fall open enrollment period. This is the most important document you will receive from Medicare. The ANOC will detail every modification to your plan, including changes in the following:

- Service area
- Coverage
- Premiums
- Copays
- Deductibles

If you don't receive an ANOC, contact the provider. You can't make an informed choice without this document.

Check On Your Providers

Just because your doctors and other healthcare professionals participated in your plan last year, that does not mean they will do so this year. The lists of participating and in-network providers changes often, and that can make a huge difference in your coverage and copays. You'll also want to make sure the doctors you choose accept the Medicare-approved fee (called "assignment") as full payment. Doctors who don't accept assignment may charge you additional out-of-pocket fees for their services.

Take Advantage of Freebies

Medicare plans offer tons of free services that many people don't know about. Most health screenings (including mental health) are free. You may also be eligible for free stop-smoking services and vaccines. Specific Part C plans may offer additional freebies like gym memberships, for example. Look at your plan details so you don't miss out on any free services.

REVIEW YOUR PART D PLAN

Medicare Part D (prescription drug) plans change frequently, and sometimes in the middle of plan years. To ensure that you're choosing the best plan, make sure that the specific medications *and dosages* you take are explicitly covered. If you decide to switch plans, you don't need to "quit" the old plan. Medicare will automatically disenroll you from your old plan when your new coverage starts.

Read the ANOC (Annual Notice of Changes)

Like Part C plans, Part D providers are required to mail out ANOCs every September. These documents will spell out any changes to the plan, so you can decide whether it still meets your needs. The most important information to check here is whether the medications you take will still be covered by this plan. Your plan will probably change its formulary (the list of drugs it covers) every year, dropping some prescription medications, adding others, and switching some to generic coverage only.

The plan may also change the rules for some drugs. For example, a medication that didn't require pre-authorization last year may require it now. Other changes may include quantity limits or "step therapy" (insisting you try a cheaper version of a drug before trying a more expensive version, even if your doctor prescribed the more expensive one).

The Shrinking (Sort of) Gap

For decades, seniors with Medicare Part D were plagued by a huge coverage gap called "the Part D donut hole." When they hit that gap, they had to pay 100 percent for all of their prescriptions until they got to the other side. In theory, that gap no longer exists for brand-name drugs and is set to disappear for generic drugs as well. In reality, though, there's still a gaping (but shallower) hole that can leave you paying more than you'd expect for your prescriptions depending on the Part D plan you choose.

Here's how it works: If your plan has a deductible, you could be faced with paying full price for your prescriptions until you reach it. Once you hit the deductible, you start paying a portion (usually 25 percent) of your drug costs. That lasts until you fall into the gap, meaning you've tapped out your plan benefits (at $3,820 for 2019) and will have to pay a much greater share of your medication costs.

The other side of that gap is called "catastrophic coverage." Once your out-of-pocket spending for prescriptions hits a preset limit ($5,100 for 2019), catastrophic coverage takes over. The plan goes back to picking up the lion's share of prescription costs, up to 95 percent.

Some Part D plans offer extra coverage through that gap. Others offer special pricing for specific medications. If you expect to have heavy prescription drugs costs, taking the time to find a plan that matches your situation can greatly reduce your out-of-pocket spending.

Automatic Re-Enrollment

If you decide to keep the same plan you used last year, you don't have to do anything. Medicare will automatically re-enroll you in whatever coverage you had before, as long as that plan still exists. That doesn't mean your premiums, copays, and deductibles will stay the same, though, so make sure you know what will change even if you don't change plans.

Chapter 7

New Trends in Retirement

The world is changing rapidly, and retirement is moving right along with it. People are reshaping how retirement works, what it looks like, and how to customize it. Most important, the biggest new trend in retirement is flexibility. Retirees have to be able to pivot and adapt to balance extended longevity with constantly shifting economic conditions. Whatever your retirement ends up looking like, it almost certainly won't match up with the pension-gold watch-golfing model that was the norm fifty years ago.

THE FIRE MOVEMENT

Catch Financial Independence Fever

The Financial Independence/Retire Early, or FIRE, movement has gained a lot of momentum, appealing to people in their thirties and forties. After all, both parts sound great. And while the name includes the word "retirement," it's more about living flexibly, and charting the course for your life without having to constantly worry about money. In fact, FIRE enthusiasts often do work, but out of choice rather than necessity.

The key philosophy here is maximizing the gap between what you earn and what you spend, allowing for accelerated savings. The bigger the gap, the more quickly you'll achieve FIRE status. Starting early brings another huge advantage here; the sooner you start ultra-saving, the more your money will grow itself through compounding.

How do you know when you've achieved financial independence and can retire early? There are different guideposts out there, but basically once you've saved up twenty-five to thirty years of living expenses, you're FIRE-ready. For example, if you have annual living expenses of $50,000 per year, you'll be financially independent when your nest egg has grown to be between $1,250,000 (50,000 × 25) to $1,500,000 (50,000 × 30). Once you hit your savings goal, you can maintain your FIRE lifestyle by withdrawing around 3 percent to 4 percent of the principal every year.

DIFFERENT FIRE STYLES

The loudest voices in the FIRE movement preach ultrafrugal living, but that lifestyle doesn't work for everyone. That's why there are a few different FIRE styles, though we mainly hear only about the extreme cost-cutting version. If living on a shoestring budget doesn't appeal to you, look into the other types to find one that better fits with your lifestyle and life goals.

Lean FIRE

The Lean FIRE strategy is the one that gets the most press; It's the version that calls for cutting expenses to the bone. Lean FIRE enthusiasts live extremely frugally, banking and investing as much as 70 percent to 80 percent of their yearly income. They invest that money carefully (maximizing returns and minimizing fees) in order to take full advantage of the power of compounding to supercharge their nest eggs. Once the savings goal is met, followers of the Lean FIRE philosophy continue to live very frugal lifestyles. Basically, every time you cut your monthly expenses by $50, you shave $15,000 off of your required nest egg ($50 × 12 = $600; $600 × 25 years = $15,000).

Living Lean can be tough if you have family to support, health issues, or fixed financial obligations. You may not be able to keep expenses down to 30 percent of income, but you can still create a sizeable nest egg by saving 35 percent to 50 percent.

Fat FIRE

With this version, you live a sensible, intentional spending life—not cutting costs to the bone but not splurging on every whim. The goal here is to prioritize income and to save a larger portion of your income than the average person to build up a significant nest egg in a fairly short period of time. This strategy works for people who don't fully buy into the minimalist movement and extreme cost-cutting style, but want to enjoy financial independence.

With the Fat FIRE approach, you'll still pay careful attention to what you're spending money on, just not to the point where it interferes with enjoying your life. That doesn't mean splurging on sports cars and impromptu island vacations; rather it means spending money intentionally on the things you truly need and want without being wasteful. Still, maintaining a nonfrugal lifestyle costs more, which means you'll need to have a bigger nest egg to get to FIRE.

Barista FIRE

The aim of the Barista FIRE plan is a large degree of financial independence. Part of your support comes from savings, and the balance comes from a part-time job where you work enough hours to score some benefits (like health insurance). Along with the financial benefits of a job, many people choose this strategy for the continued social interactions and because they enjoy working. The "FI" (Financial Independence) part means that they're financially independent enough to not *need* to keep the job if they don't like it.

Under this FIRE strategy, you still want to save twenty-five or thirty years' worth of expenses; just because you plan to work doesn't mean you'll be able to find work. This allows you more freedom to choose a job you enjoy, stretch your savings further, and splurge when you want to because there's still income coming in.

FIRE PILLARS

The FIRE movement stands on three main pillars: reduce spending, boost income, and invest wisely. In the most basic terms, it's the classic budget mantra: Spend less than you earn and bank the rest. By increasing earnings and cutting costs at the same time, you'll have more money available to put toward your FIRE nest egg.

Reduce Spending

Regardless of the FIRE style, spending money carefully and with intention is a key facet of the plan. A focus on reducing the biggest expenses helps trim spending further and faster than cutting small everyday expenses, but even those smaller expenses can add up. Pay attention to the purpose of your purchases, and whether or not they're necessary to you. In other words, if your goal is to achieve financial independence as soon as possible, don't spend money on "wants" and minimize (or at least lower) spending on necessities.

To reduce your living expenses and achieve financial independence, follow these guidelines:

- Reduce housing costs (usually the single largest expenditure), which includes all associated expenses from rent or mortgage to utility bills.
- Buy only used cars.
- Use rewards points whenever possible, such as funding out-of-budget purchases.
- Lower your income tax bill by contributing as much as possible to tax-advantaged accounts (such as IRAs and HSAs).
- Shop around for the least expensive cell phone, Internet, and streaming services.

Boost Income

On the other side, increased income also presents more opportunity for savings. While you're in FIRE-prep mode, find ways to bring in more money and set up as many income streams as you can. No matter how much you're earning, find a way to earn more. That can involve getting a raise at your current job, taking on a second job or a side hustle (or two), and setting up a series of passive income streams. Every extra dollar of earnings goes straight into your FIRE nest egg (after you've totally maxed out contributions to every possible tax-advantaged retirement savings account).

Passive Income Streams

When you earn money without ongoing effort (or at least not much effort), that's a passive income stream. Examples include investment earnings, rent from rental real estate, royalties, and ad money from a website. Passive income streams don't appear overnight; they take plenty of work on the front end, so you can enjoy effortless income on the backend.

Invest Wisely

FIRE-starters will make the most of their money by investing in growth-oriented low- or no-cost ETFs (exchange-traded funds) and index mutual funds. These investment choices offer plenty in the way of diversification and strong returns that won't be eaten away by fund fees.

Because investing always comes with the risk of loss, keep around two years' worth of expenses in 100 percent safe options like FDIC-insured bank accounts (which can be money market accounts or short-term CDs). The rest stays in the most aggressive funds you can stomach for maximum growth potential.

MULTIGENERATION PLANS

The New Old Normal

For centuries, having many generations living in a single household was the norm; it still is in many cultures. This old family-style living arrangement is once again gaining ground in the US. Around 20 percent of Americans—64 million people—now live in multigenerational homes, according to the Pew Research Center. That number includes 28.4 million three-generation households. Though often this involves adult children (aged twenty-five and older) moving back into their parents' homes, the number of older adults (aged fifty-five and older) moving in with their children has increased as well.

MULTIGENERATION LIVING

The number of multigenerational households has grown rapidly as it's become more common for parents to live with their (adult) children. This situation may be born out of financial necessity or because aging parents can't (or don't want to) live on their own. Whatever the motivation, adding more people into a single household changes the family finances and the family dynamic. Going into it with a clear plan will help ease some of the adjustment pains, especially when it comes to money.

Sharing Costs

Creating a family budget is the best way to reduce financial friction when you have multiple generations of adults living in the same household. This helps track common expenses (like utilities) and individual expenses (like food for special diets) so you can work out a cost-sharing arrangement that everyone can live with. Keep in mind that while the rent or mortgage payment won't change, other housing-related expenses (like electric and water) will increase. Be clear up front about how expenses will be shared, and whose responsibility it will be to manage the family cash flow (which could possibly be more than one person).

Sharing Space

Creating a "space budget" can also help keep your home running more smoothly. Work out in advance which areas of the house will be for common use and specify where each member has private space.

Other issues to add to your space budget include the following:

- Setting bathroom schedules
- Sharing kitchen space
- Giving notice for guests and entertaining
- Anticipating noise issues
- Designating chores

It's hard to balance everyone's needs and very common to prioritize others' needs over your own. Setting clear ground rules from day one will make sure that no one's needs get overlooked.

MULTIGENERATION
FINANCIAL PLANNING

There's a lot of wealth concentrated inside (and outside) retirement accounts. To preserve the family nest egg, it pays to engage in multigeneration financial planning. This goes beyond the scope of standard personal financial planning to consider children, grandchildren, and possibly parents. Without proper planning, an outsized portion of that wealth could be lost to taxes.

Estate Tax and Inheritance Tax

Estate tax and inheritance tax are two different things. Estate tax gets levied based on the total value of an estate (which includes homes, retirement plans, investments, etc.) after someone dies but before assets are transferred to heirs. Inheritance tax (still charged by a handful of states) kicks in after heirs receive estate assets, depending on the total amount each heir inherited.

Meshing Your Financial Plan with Your Estate Plan

You go to a financial professional for your financial plan and a lawyer for your estate plan, but that can leave the two working against each other. Your financial plan focuses on building up assets, while your estate plan spells out your wishes for how those assets will be eventually distributed. If you've accumulated substantial assets, you'll want to transfer them in the most direct, tax-efficient way to preserve that wealth for your family. The specifics will depend on your situation, but may involve a combination of planned gifting, family trusts, and direct transfers. Direct transfers include things like designating bank or brokerage accounts as "transfer on death" (TOD) and naming beneficiaries. Make sure the professional helping you with your estate planning understands your financial plan, and that your financial planner understands your intentions for transferring assets.

WORKING RETIREMENT

The Jumbo Shrimp of Life

It sounds like an oxymoron, but working retirements are becoming the norm. Whether you take a downsized position with your current employer, pursue a different career, or start that business you've been thinking about for years, there are many advantages to keeping at least one foot in the working world. While the most obvious benefit is the paycheck and possibly the ability to hold on to other benefits—such as a 401(k) plan, health insurance, and employee discounts—you'll also stay socially and mentally engaged. If you can't picture yourself not working, pursuing one of these on-the-job retirement strategies could be just right for you.

PHASED RETIREMENT

A phased retirement involves gradually transitioning from a full-time position to full-time retirement without changing employers. This helps workers avoid the sudden shock of a major life transition and helps the employer maintain more continuity in the workplace. While the vast majority of employers agree that this type of plan makes sense, only 31 percent of companies actually offer some sort of formal phased retirement plan (according to the Transamerica Center for Retirement Studies). If you want to pursue a phased retirement but your employer doesn't offer that option, ask about it anyway—maybe suggest a trial period to see how it works for both of you.

Phased retirement doesn't come in a one-size-fits-all plan. There are many ways to implement a more gradual departure from the workplace and the attached paycheck and benefits. This could include the following:

- Negotiating a reduced work schedule (fewer hours or days per week)
- Taking on part-time work
- Job sharing
- Shifting job responsibilities (from production toward training, for example)
- Working from home

Since there's no fixed definition of phased retirement, employers have complete flexibility to design the plan that works best for the particular position.

Examples of existing programs (according to the US Government Accountability Office) include reducing hours and pay by 20 percent while allowing employees to keep accrued pension benefits and health insurance; switching to less complex or stressful responsibilities; or transitioning to part-time schedules where employees work at least twenty-five hours per week to maintain health insurance.

ENCORE CAREERS

If the idea of full retirement doesn't suit you, but you don't want to work at your longtime job anymore, consider pursuing an encore career. Whether you've always dreamed of devoting more time to important issues or public service, turning a favorite hobby into a money-making venture, or using your skills and talents in a different way, there's a "second act" for you.

What Have You Always Wanted to Do?

It can be tough to figure out the right encore career for you, but it all starts with what you truly dream about doing. Here, identifying the "why" is as important as the "what," and can help you clarify the role you want to play moving forward. If there's not a clear, straight path to your second-act dream job, map out the steps you'd need to take to get there.

If you loved what you've been doing but just need a change of pace, think about going into consulting or coaching. This lets you build on connections you've made during your prime working years and continue capitalizing on your existing skill set. With yourself in the driver's seat, you can choose which gigs you want to take, when you want to work, and what any workday will look like. You'll have the flexibility and freedom of retirement combined with the ability to earn money and feel purposeful.

Giving Back

Nonprofit organizations are among the most common post-retirement work destinations. You can still employ your well-developed skills for a paycheck (usually a much smaller paycheck) and devote time and energy to a cause you believe in. This is not the same as volunteering; it's a regular job with associated responsibilities and pay.

There are many online resources available for seniors seeking encore careers in the public service and nonprofit sectors, including the following:

- ReServe.org, www.reserveinc.org
- Encore.org, www.encore.org

- Executive Service Corps, www.escus.org
- Idealist.org, www.idealist.org
- WorkforGood.org, www.workforgood.org

Service Plus

You can combine your desire to serve with something you love to do to double up on the benefits. Love going to shows? Volunteer as an usher at the theater. Love museums? Sign up as a tour guide. There are many volunteer opportunities that let you enjoy your time while you give back. Consider volunteering at aquariums, libraries, zoos, or national parks—whatever matches your interests.

Pursuing a Passion

Always wanted to open your own bakery...bike shop...garden design business? Thought about turning a longtime hobby into a late-life moneymaker? Post-retirement is a great time to pursue a potentially profitable passion. These encores may entail some education, training, or licensing, and they all require careful planning. If you've never launched a business before, especially one that involves a sizeable cash outlay, take the time to do some research and create a formal business plan (even if it's just for you) before you dive in. It can take time (often years, maybe never) to start turning a profit with a small business; make sure your finances can handle the potential losses before you get started.

If you need help turning your ideas into plans, you can connect with a Service Corps of Retired Executives (SCORE) mentor by visiting www.score.org. You can also find a wealth of resources, including detailed business plan templates and financing sources, at the US Small Business Administration at www.sba.gov.

UPSIZING VERSUS DOWNSIZING

Choose Your Own Adventure

Retirement often sparks substantial change apart from the change in work. With financial independence and an abundance of free time, retirees often embark on new life journeys. Some break free and live large after a lifetime of saving up; others devote their time to home, family, and friends. Whether you decide to go big or pare down, make sure you're financially prepared for your new life.

UPSIZING

The upsized retirement movement has two branches: one is literally getting a bigger (i.e., more square feet) home, and the other is pursuing luxury living. After a lifetime of saving and sacrificing, many seniors want to treat themselves and live the way they want to while they can.

You might guess that both of those branches cost much more than a traditional retirement, but that's not always the case. In fact, some (but definitely not all) of the upsize strategies can result in reduced monthly expenses.

Going Bigger

While around half of retirees buy smaller homes, nearly a third upsize and move into larger homes. According to a Merrill Lynch and Age Wave Survey, the number one reason for going bigger in retirement is starting a business, followed by wanting more room for family and friends to visit, or for family to be able to move in. In addition, larger homes make it easier to age in place, especially in the face of failing health; there's more room to accommodate live-in help. Plus, as a side bonus, having more space can be beneficial for spouses who aren't used to being around each other all the time.

Going bigger doesn't always mean going more expensive. Moving to a low cost-of-living area might allow you to buy a much bigger house for less money than you'll get for your current house. Even if that's the case, though, larger houses typically cost more for ongoing expenses, including insurance, property taxes, utilities, and maintenance. Make sure your budget can handle all of the costs of upsizing before you buy.

Hit the High Seas

If you love traveling and adventure, retiring on a cruise ship might be a great option for you. Not only do you get to see the world and visit exotic ports of call, you also could help your retirement savings last longer. This new entry in the retirement category features all-inclusive fares (food, housekeeping services, fitness centers, etc.) that run the range from economy to luxury. Seniors also score all kinds of discounts by booking extended trips (which last for months as opposed to days). Now, as millions of baby boomers slide into retirement, retirement-specific cruise options have begun to crop up. Some mirror life in a landside retirement community, while others stick to more traditional cruise patterns (think *Love Boat*). If a life on the high seas appeals to you, check out Senior Living at Sea (https://cruiseweb.com/senior-living-at-sea).

Some things to think about if you choose to retire on a cruise ship:

- Medicare won't cover you outside the US, or while you're at sea if you're more than six hours away from the closest US port.
- You can't bring pets on a cruise (in most cases).
- Extras (like entertainment while at port) can quickly chip away at your retirement nest egg.
- You'll have to make long-term arrangements for things like collecting your mail, paying your taxes, paying bills, and banking (which is necessary for your RMDs and Social Security checks).

DOWNSIZING

The vast majority of retirees downsize once (or even before) they stop working, and that move comes with a lot of benefits. Not only does it reduce monthly expenses, which helps stretch retirement savings further. It also makes life easier: less space to clean, less maintenance, and simpler living. Though your house will be your home base, going small creates an opening to spend big on extras like travel, entertainment, and grandkids (which are among the biggest retirement budget busters).

Beware These Downsizing Downsides

For many retirees, the point of downsizing is to sell their house, buy a smaller house, and come out of the transactions with a sizeable chunk of cash to add to their nest egg. Unfortunately, things don't always work out that way. Here are some ways you can maximize your chance of success and avoid some common pitfalls that may knock your plan off course:

- Find out how much your home can sell for realistically. Start on websites like *Zillow* (www.zillow.com) or Realtor.com (www .realtor.com). Check with at least two realtors to see how they'd price your property. And don't make high-cost renovations that won't add enough to the sales price.
- Don't underestimate the cost of your new home, especially if you're moving to a new area. Spend time looking around to get a feel for the neighborhood and a good sense of current home values. Check online resources like *Zillow* and Realtor.com to see what similar homes are selling for in your target buying zone.
- Account for closing costs for both deals. You'll most likely have to shell out closing costs when you sell your old house and when you buy your new house, and that can really add up. Do what you can to lower those costs, like negotiating the commission with your realtor or asking the seller of the home you're buying to pick up some of the closing costs (which the people buying your house will probably ask of you).

You'll also want to make sure you can easily cover all of the monthly costs associated with the new house, especially if you're downsizing because you can't afford your current home.

Granny Pods

For people who want to be close to family in retirement without actually living together, granny pods may offer the perfect middle ground. These tiny homes are backyard guesthouses that are specifically equipped to meet seniors' special needs and can be adapted with medical equipment if necessary. Averaging around 400 square feet, granny pods have everything regular houses have, just on a smaller scale. These single-level homes come with doorways and hallways that are wide enough for wheelchairs (just in case), walk-in showers, and many are equipped with smart home features. Plus, granny pods are mobile, so they can come along if the family moves.

Cost-wise, granny pods range from $37,000 to more than $125,000, based on their size and any extras (like medical equipment, for example). These homes are not eligible for mortgages, so you have to pay the whole amount up front. Plus, granny pods share utilities and water with the main house, which will lead to an increase in those bills.

The Freedom of Small

While many people associate downsizing with sacrificing, it's often incredibly freeing, both emotionally and financially. With fewer fixed expenses hanging over your head, financial stress will ease. And as financial stress has been linked with some serious physical and emotional health issues, reducing it can have a very positive impact on your life.

HOMESHARING

The *Golden Girls* Alternative

When you don't want to live alone, but you don't want to leave your house, think about homesharing. You'll get extra cash to help cover your monthly expenses, help with housekeeping chores, and another person around for both social and security reasons. In exchange for a private bedroom and some shared common space, the tenant provides some combination of rent and services (like household help or transportation, for example) based on what works best for your situation.

So many seniors are choosing this option that nonprofits have cropped up around the country to help make good (and safe) matches. Whether you're looking for another retiree or someone younger who can help out with more physically demanding chores, homesharing can benefit both of you.

KNOW WHAT YOU'RE LOOKING FOR

Once you've decided to give homesharing a try, figure out exactly what you want in a housemate (whether you're the host or the guest).

Important Factors to Consider

Living with a new person is hard, especially at first. To give your homesharing arrangement the best possible chance of success, it's important to think about the qualities you want in your housemate, the things you can tolerate, and those you absolutely cannot accept.

Ask yourself these important questions if you are considering a homesharing arrangement:

- Do you want to share a bathroom?
- Are you comfortable with pets?
- Are you looking for companionship?
- What types of chores do you need done or are you willing to do?
- What's your mess tolerance?
- What are your dealbreakers?

Be completely honest with yourself and any homesharing service you use or in any profile you create. If you tend to be messy or noisy, say so; your housemate will find out, and it's better to be upfront about anything that could put a crimp in the relationship.

Give It Time and Patience

If you've never had an unrelated housemate before, or if you've been living on your own for a long time, it can feel awkward to suddenly have a virtual stranger living with you. No matter what your expectations are for the housemate relationship, it will take time to get there. No matter how perfect the match, be prepared for a lengthy adjustment period. You'll have to get used to each other's quirks and habits, schedule (early riser or night owl, for example), and dozens of minor annoyances. Be prepared for disputes—any two people living together are bound to butt heads on occasion.

FINDING YOUR HOUSEMATE

Once you've decided you want to share a home, whether you'll be the landlord or the tenant, you'll want to find the best possible roommate.

Local Homeshare Programs

All across the country, local homeshare programs help match homeowners with renters. These primarily nonprofit groups screen and interview all prospects. They may do a home visit to make sure the accommodations are suitable. Some programs check references, and some even require fingerprint checks. Once that's done and they think two prospects would make a good match, the homeshare program connects them (this can take weeks or even months). After they meet and decide to move forward, the group helps draw up a detailed rental agreement; these agreements get down into the details, like listing quiet times and how food will be shared or separated.

To find a nonprofit homeshare program near you, visit the National Shared Housing Resource Center website at www .nationalsharedhousing.org. The site has a comprehensive listing of programs by state (though not every state has local programs).

Try an Online Matchmaker

Online homesharing matchmakers work more like dating apps: You fill out a detailed profile, and the service returns potential matches. These programs do not typically run background checks or interview the people listed on their sites; that part is up to you. You'll also need to come up with your own lease agreement, though some sites offer state-specific lease templates. Plus, since these match-makers are for-profit businesses, you may have to pay a fee to use the sites. They may also offer add-on services (such as background checks) for additional fees.

While people of any age can post their profiles, these sites cater primarily to adults over age fifty and retirees. Secure, reputable online matching services include Silvernest (www.silvernest.com) and Senior Homeshares (www.seniorhomeshares.com).

Check Your Homeowners Policy

Typical homeowners insurance policies do not cover renters, and that may include homesharing "guests." When you open your home to a housemate, you're taking on extra liability, so you need the right insurance coverage to protect your home and your nest egg. Check with your insurance provider to see whether you need to update your policy.

Chapter 8

Tricky Situations and FAQs

Although a lot of the moving pieces of retirement are confusing, some take complications to the next level. It can be very tough to make sense of some of these issues, and looking for answers on the web can jumble things even more. The truth is, at least one of these will affect you at some point. By understanding the basics of how each can affect your retirement, you'll be better prepared to come through financially unscathed, and maybe in even better shape than you were before.

ANNUITIES (DON'T SKIP THIS SECTION!)

Make Your Own Pension

There may be no financial term that prompts as much contempt as annuities—but that's because most people (including the people selling them) don't understand how they really work. The right annuity can be a retirement lifesaver, providing a *guaranteed* income stream that's unaffected by market ups and downs.

A DIY PENSION

When it's set up and used properly, an annuity supplies guaranteed steady income for life. The right annuity gives you a reliable monthly income stream that you know you can count on forever, no matter what happens in the economy or the stock market. That's especially valuable for people who don't have pensions, and rely only on Social Security for guaranteed income.

Annuity Basics

Annuities are insurance products (which is why they're often sold by insurance salespeople). You buy (or invest in) an annuity, and the annuity pays you regularly in the future. You can set up your annuity to make monthly, quarterly, or annual payments, or get the money in a lump sum at a specified future date.

The amount of each payment depends on several factors, including the size of the annuity, how the payments are scheduled, and for how long the payments will be made. You'll also have the option to receive payments for a certain number of years or for the rest of your life.

The Tax Advantage of Annuities

Like retirement accounts, the money inside an annuity grows tax-deferred. That allows for more compounding power, so your nest egg can grow more quickly. You don't pay any taxes on the earnings until you start taking the payouts. At that time, only the earnings portion of the payments gets taxed at your regular income tax rate; you already paid income taxes on the money you used to open the annuity, so there's no more tax to pay there.

Unlike retirement accounts, there's no limit on the amount of money you can contribute to an annuity, either annually or over your lifetime. Because of the unlimited contribution feature, an annuity can be an excellent tool for people who fall behind on retirement savings early on and want to do as much as they can to catch up when they have the cash to do that.

CHOOSING THE RIGHT
ANNUITY FOR YOU

The key to annuity success lies in knowing what you want *before* you start to shop. Annuities can get super complicated very quickly—especially if you buy one through an insurance broker. Salespeople have lots of bells and whistles to offer, and they normally get more commission for each feature you add on. Those features will sound amazing, and it's easy to get caught up in the hype, but most of them will not add any value for you.

You can avoid the sales pitch by choosing a direct-sold annuity. These are available from many investment companies, including Fidelity (www.fidelity.com), Vanguard (www.vanguard.com), and Charles Schwab (www.schwab.com). These annuities typically come with lower fees than those sold by insurance brokers.

Annuity Framework

There are a lot of different twists on annuities, and new ones can pop up at any time. But at heart, annuities come with two main choices: deferred versus immediate, and fixed versus variable. You can mix and match those choices (such as an immediate, fixed annuity) depending on what works for your situation. Here's a closer look at what those labels really mean:

- Deferred annuities keep your money invested for a set time period until you're ready to receive payments.
- Immediate annuities start sending payments right after you invest in them.
- Fixed annuities offer guaranteed payments, where you get a specific dollar amount for a set period of time.
- Variable annuities deliver payments based on the performance of underlying investments.

Once you have the framework for your annuity, there are many special features—called riders—that you could add. Riders add cost, and those costs can really accumulate. And, honestly, most of the riders will not benefit you as much as it sounds like they will.

Know Your Payment Options

When you buy an annuity, you get to choose what your payments will look like once they start. There are a few different main choices:

- **Period certain:** You choose a specific number of years over which the annuity will pay out (usually ten, fifteen, or twenty years). If you die before that time is up, your beneficiary will get the remaining payments.
- **Lifetime payments:** This offers a guaranteed payment (based on your life expectancy) for as long as you live; when you die, the payments stop cold (this is sometimes called the single life option). If you're worried about outliving your money, this option might make sense for you.
- **Joint life option:** This option (also called joint and survivor) offers guaranteed payments for life for whoever lives longer, you or your spouse (if you die, your spouse keeps getting the payments). Payments are usually smaller than the lifetime payment option because they are calculated based on your and your spouse's joint life expectancy.
- **Life with guaranteed term:** This option combines the lifetime and period-certain styles. You're guaranteed payments for life, plus a special guaranteed period (usually ten years) during which your spouse will continue to get payments if you die before the period expires.

Keep an Eagle Eye on Expenses

Annuities are notorious for having high and sometimes hidden expenses. Those fees can greatly eat away at any profits building up inside the annuity, so be aware of every charge in your contract. The different types of annuities come with some different fees.

Deferred annuities come with surrender charges, which are sort of like early withdrawal penalties. You'll pay a surrender fee if you take any money out within the first several years of the contract. Surrender charges start out high (sometimes super high, like 20 percent) and decrease annually until they hit zero. (Immediate annuities don't have surrender charges because you're supposed to start getting payments immediately.) Variable annuities come with ongoing maintenance expenses, which normally include insurance charges (remember, annuities are insurance products) and investment management fees.

Beware Tax Penalties

Because annuities act like retirement accounts where you don't pay income taxes on the earnings inside the annuity, you have to wait until you reach age fifty-nine-and-a-half to take the money out. If you take any withdrawals before then, they'll be subject to a 10 percent tax penalty in addition to any regular income taxes.

REVERSE MORTGAGES

Homeowners Beware

Reverse mortgages are tricky. They sound like easy money: getting (instead of making) monthly payments for your house without having to sell it. But the truth about reverse mortgages is much more complicated. Use extreme caution when considering this option, because it comes with a devastating downside: losing your home and gutting your nest egg. There are some limited situations where a reverse mortgage can be beneficial, but those are not the norm.

Scam Alert

Reverse mortgages offer big rewards for lenders, so the industry is full of scams. Dishonest vendors (and sometimes even greedy family members) purposely target financially vulnerable seniors and convince them to take out damaging loans. If anyone approaches you about a reverse mortgage, run the other way.

HOW REVERSE MORTGAGES WORK

Reverse mortgages work sort of like home equity loans that you don't have to pay back right away. Basically, you take a piece of your equity (the amount of your home that you own 100 percent free and clear) and trade it for regular monthly income payments—almost like an advance on eventually selling your house. Whenever you do sell the house, you pay off the loan plus interest. The loan will also come due in full if you die or move out of the house (even if other people still live there).

Unlike regular mortgage loans where the balance decreases with every payment, reverse mortgages increase over time. Eventually, you'll have to pay back every penny you got plus years' worth of interest.

Three Main Types

All reverse mortgages follow the same basic plan. They're available for homeowners who are at least sixty-two years old and own most or all of their home (with no outstanding loans or liens). The home has to be the primary residence (you have to live there). And you can't have any federal outstanding debts (like back taxes). However, the three main types of these loans come with their own unique twists.

The Federal Housing Administration (FHA) offers its own brand of reverse mortgages called home equity conversion mortgages (HECMs). Only homes valued below a government-set cap qualify for these loans (so if you have a high-value home, it may not make the cut). These loans are federally insured, and the proceeds can be used for any purpose. Potential borrowers are required to meet with HUD-certified reverse mortgage counselors to make sure they understand all of the loan details and potential consequences.

Proprietary reverse mortgages are loans from private companies. People with high-priced homes can get bigger loans with this type. And because there's no government involvement, you may not be required to get mortgage insurance. Use extra caution with these loans, though, because they aren't handcuffed by federal regulations and may have more requirements and restrictions for keeping loans in good standing. Plus, they may loan you *more* than your equity, which could leave you in dire financial straits if the loan were to suddenly come due.

Single-use reverse mortgages do just what their name spells out: How the proceeds can be used is up to the lender, not the borrower (you). Often, these loans can be used only for home-related expenses, like paying property taxes or making home repairs. Many states and nonprofit organizations offer these loans to help struggling homeowners stay in their homes.

Before you commit to any reverse mortgage, talk with an experienced HECM counselor even if you're not getting an official HECM loan. They will explain the benefits and drawbacks, compare the fees and costs of different loans, and help you understand all the terms and conditions of any loan you're considering. You can find a list of qualified counselors at www.hud.gov.

Fees, Fees, and More Fees

No matter what kind of reverse mortgage you get, you will be paying fees, and plenty of them. The standard fees include the following:

- Origination fees (the charge to create the loan)
- Closing costs (just like with a regular mortgage)
- Servicing fees (annual or monthly fees over the life of the loan)
- Mortgage insurance premiums (that protect the lender against losses)

Those are the basic fees, but some reverse mortgage lenders bundle in even more fees (even if they don't explicitly call them "fees").

WATCH OUT FOR THESE PERILOUS PITFALLS

Ideally, you'd take out a reverse mortgage to boost your monthly income. A few years later, you'd sell your house, get a windfall, pay off the reverse mortgage, and have plenty of cash to spare. More often, though, that's not what happens.

There are a lot of ways these loans can turn ugly. When that happens, you will lose your house and probably a great deal of money. It's crucial that you know ahead of time all the ways that you could be forced to leave your home because of the reverse mortgage.

You Can Change Your Mind

After you sign a reverse mortgage contract, you have at least three business days to change your mind. If you do, notify the lender in writing (not email). Send the letter by certified mail with a return receipt, and keep that documentation in your records. Once you cancel, the lender has to return any money you've paid within twenty days.

You Can't Afford the Upkeep

Reverse mortgage contracts are very strict about keeping up with all of your home-related payments, which include:

- Property taxes
- Homeowners insurance (which you are required to have)
- Homeowners association dues
- Basic home maintenance

Depending on the contract, missing even a single one of those payments or failing to keep up with the yard work can result in the lender calling in the loan. If you don't have enough cash to pay back the full loan with interest, you'll be forced to sell or endure foreclosure.

You Leave the Home

Reverse mortgages come with another very strict rule: *You*, the named borrower, *must be living in the home*. If you don't live there for more than one year (which can happen for medical reasons, such as long-term rehab for a hip fracture), the loan must be repaid. If you take a thirteen-month world cruise, the loan must be repaid. If you die, and yours is the only name on the loan contract, the loan must be repaid immediately.

When the loan has to be repaid, it almost always involves selling the house and handing over a huge chunk of the proceeds to the lender. Unless there's another source of funds that can be used to pay the loan, your spouse, children, roommate, or anyone else living in the house will almost certainly have to move out.

AVOID FRAUD, SCAMS, AND TRAPS

Trust Your Spidey Senses

Sad but true: Retirement savings and retirees are among the largest targets for scam artists. Even a single encounter with these fraudsters can wipe out your retirement savings before you realize it. Unfortunately, family members often fall into this category, taking advantage of strong savers in a variety of perfectly legal ways. And even well-intentioned family members can drain your retirement savings or keep you from putting away enough money for your financial future.

Saving for retirement is hard enough without encountering fraud and money traps. That's why it's crucial to take decisive steps to invest safely, protect your nest egg, and prioritize your future self.

WATCH OUT FOR INVESTMENT SCAMS

Fraudsters know that people are freaked out about having enough money saved for retirement, and they profit by preying on those fears. These con artists will look and sound professional, delivering polished presentations with "proof" of guaranteed returns or "once in a lifetime" opportunities to earn returns higher than the market average. Regardless of how you were introduced to the salesperson, even if you know someone who says they've made money with this investment, stay skeptical until you've done your homework.

Know the Red Flags

It's not always easy to spot investment scams. That's especially true when you're already feeling anxious about your retirement savings. Con artists know exactly how to tap into your biggest fears about financial security, and they will use those fears to steal your money. While it's important to always take your time when considering investments, walk away immediately if you spot any of the following red flags:

- Phrases like "guaranteed returns," "never run out of money," or "risk-free"
- Free travel, meals, or seminars
- Penny stocks
- Confusing or complex explanations
- Lots of hype with few details
- Unsolicited emails or cold calls
- Pressure to make a hasty, unplanned investment

If you spot any of these red flags or in any way suspect someone is trying to con you, file a complaint. You can report your suspicions to the US Securities and Exchange Commission (SEC) at www.sec.gov or to the Financial Industry Regulatory Authority (FINRA, at www.finra.org).

Take These Steps to Protect Your Nest Egg

Never—*never*—invest in something that you don't fully understand. Be skeptical when someone is working overtime to sell you something, or pressuring you into acting quickly (as in, "before it's too late"). Ask questions, and verify the answers independently.

Take these steps to confirm that you're dealing with a legit sales-person and investment:

1. Verify the salesperson's credentials. Make sure they are a legally licensed investment broker by searching for them on BrokerCheck (https://brokercheck.finra.org).
2. Check with your state's securities regulator to see if any complaints have been filed; you can find their contact information on the North American Securities Administrators Association site (NASAA, at www.nasaa.org).
3. Look into the company's background along with current and historical financial statements through the SEC's online database (called EDGAR) by visiting www.sec.gov. Do not rely on documents provided by the salesperson; do your own digging.

Shocking Statistics

In 2018, according to the Federal Trade Commission (FTC), 1.4 million people reported being victims of fraud. An additional 444,000 people were victims of identity theft. Overall, people lost $1.48 *billion* to fraud. Adults over age sixty lost the most money both individually and as a group, accounting for nearly 40 percent of the total losses.

SENIOR-TARGETING SCAMS

Criminals swindle seniors in dozens of ways, not just with investment scams. Crooks constantly invent new ways to target seniors. Even if you have an eye out for all of the current frauds, you may not be expecting whatever comes next. Because they're looking for quick payouts, these scammers will almost always target you by phone or email using masking technology to make it seem like the contact is coming from a legitimate source.

Suspended Social Security

One of the newer scams (according to the FTC) involves phone calls from a person who claims to work for Social Security. The call will probably *look* like it's coming from the SSA (Social Security Administration) office. That official-sounding person informs you that your Social Security number has been suspended because of suspicious activity. They offer up instructions for how to reactivate your Social Security number, such as verifying the number, confirming your contact information, and providing the information for the bank account where your benefits get deposited. They may also request that you send a reactivation fee.

If you get a similar call, hang up and call the SSA or report the call to the FTC. Real SSA employees will *never* call you and ask for your Social Security number. They won't ask you to confirm the last four digits over the phone. They will also never require you to pay a fee.

Bogus Government Officials

Con men don't just pretend to be SSA employees. They may claim to be calling from Medicare, the IRS (Internal Revenue Service), or your local court system. The calls will almost always include some kind of threat (like you will be arrested) unless you pay a fee, a tax penalty, or a fine. They'll try to trick you into revealing personal and financial information to clear up the problem. Again, hang up.

Real government agencies won't normally initiate contact by phone or email. You'll get letters through the regular mail, sometimes several, when they begin reaching out to you. Even if they do eventually call you (without it being a return call), they will never ask for personal financial information or payments over the phone.

SUPPORTING ADULT CHILDREN

Even though there's no fraud or ill-intent here, adult children who rely on parents for support are usually unwittingly undermining their parent's future financial security. More than half of older Americans support their adult children (those who are over eighteen) to the detriment of their own retirement security (according to a survey by www.bankrate.com). Another study (this one done by Merrill Lynch) found that 60 percent of parents said they would delay their retirement to support family members, including their adult children.

Parents supply money for student loan payments, groceries, rent, credit card bills, and more for their children despite the fact that they believe their children should shoulder the responsibility for their own bills.

That support cuts into money that would have been put toward retirement. In addition to underfunding their retirement, those parents are also losing out on all of the future earnings those contributions could have delivered. That puts their retirement at risk and vastly increases the chances that they'll run out of money.

It also does a disservice to the children. Forcing them to take control of their own finances (by learning to budget and finding creative ways to boost income or cut expenses, for example) will help ensure that by the time they're ready to retire, they won't be bogged down by financial stress.

DIVORCE

Going Solo

Along with the emotional and financial upset that comes with a divorce, it can also have an enormous effect on retirement savings. That's especially true if there had been a significant earnings imbalance in the relationship, such as where one spouse earned substantially more than the other or one spouse took time out of the work force to raise children.

While you're going through the divorce process, retirement will probably be the last thing on your mind—but the decisions you make now will affect your long-term financial future. What's more, the divorce rate for adults over age fifty has soared, leaving less time to recoup funds pulled from retirement accounts. Plus, as it's more expensive to support two households than one, there are usually fewer funds available to beef up retirement savings.

QDROS

Like all other assets in a divorce, retirement savings normally get divided. How the money gets split depends on a variety of factors, from the presiding state law to relative income levels.

Regardless of how the numbers work out, it's important to follow all the steps necessary to split the assets without triggering current income taxes and tax penalties, and losing a huge chunk of that money as a result.

A QDRO (Qualified Domestic Relations Order) is a special legal document that spells out how retirement plan assets will be split in a divorce. The court issues a QDRO and serves it to the employer of the spouse with the plan. That way, the spouse with the plan won't have to pay income taxes on the withdrawal. Plus, with a properly executed QDRO, the money taken out of the plan won't be subjected to the 10 percent early withdrawal penalty that normally hits premature distributions from retirement plans. And with a substantial retirement nest egg, that 10 percent could translate to an enormous amount (for example, on a $500,000 retirement account, the penalty alone would come to $50,000!).

Get the Wording Right

QDROs must contain specific information in order to be valid, so you can avoid that nasty 10-percent penalty. A proper QDRO will include the following:

- The plan owner's name and mailing address (the spouse with the account)
- The alternate payee's name and mailing address (the spouse getting the payout)
- The percentage or dollar amount of funds going to the alternate payee
- How the percentage or dollar amount was determined
- How and when the payments will be made
- How many payments will be made

You can find more details about QDRO language on the US Department of Labor website at www.dol.gov.

The Type of Plan Affects the Payout

Creating a QDRO for defined contribution plans like 401(k)s or IRAs (individual retirement accounts) is pretty straightforward. Things get more complicated when defined benefit plans are involved. The calculations for defined benefit plan payments are complex and based on a variety of factors (length of service and life expectancy, for example), so the QDRO calculations are also pretty intricate. In fact, it usually requires an actuary or other retirement benefit specialist to figure out each spouse's fair share of the plan assets. On top of that, the payout terms in the QDRO can't be different than the plan's own payout terms.

The Roth IRA Factor

When splitting retirement accounts, remember that they're not all treated the same for tax purposes. How the account will be taxed in retirement can significantly change its fair value. For example, a $50,000 Roth IRA will be worth more than a $50,000 traditional IRA because the Roth IRA funds will be tax-free during retirement and the traditional IRA funds will be taxed.

Now or Later?

Many ex-spouses who receive payouts from retirement plans don't put that money back into retirement savings; rather, they use the money to cover current expenses. If the money is not put into a retirement account, it will be subject to current income taxes (unless the money is coming out of a Roth IRA account). For example, if one spouse receives $50,000 from the other spouse's plan and doesn't roll it into a retirement account, the plan manager will automatically take 20 percent for tax purposes (sort of like withholding taxes on a paycheck). That's to cover the potential income taxes on the $50,000, which will be determined by that spouse's overall financial situation at tax time. But if that money goes straight into a retirement account, current income taxes won't apply until the money is eventually withdrawn.

That offers two important financial benefits:

1. The money will grow into a more sizeable nest egg, thanks to tax-deferred compounding.
2. Withdrawals will probably be smaller than the original lump sum, reducing the tax burden.

Plus, it would be virtually impossible to recreate that retirement savings if the money was used to pay for current expenses. Eventually saving up another $50,000 (or whatever the amount) over time won't give retirement savings the same momentum: a great deal of compounding time will be lost.

SOCIAL SECURITY AND DIVORCE

If you're divorced, you may be entitled to receive Social Security retirement benefits based on your ex-spouse's earnings. Qualifying for the benefits depends on your specific situation and whether you meet all of the following conditions:

- You're at least sixty-two years old.
- You were married for at least ten years and have been divorced for at least two years (unless your ex-spouse is already collecting Social Security benefits).
- You're not married (it doesn't matter if your ex-spouse is married).
- Your ex-spouse *qualifies* for Social Security retirement benefits (even if they haven't yet applied).
- The benefits you'd get based on your work history are less than the benefits you'd get based on your ex-spouse's work history.

If you meet all of those criteria, you'll receive up to half of your ex's full benefits. The benefits you get have no effect on the benefits that your ex-spouse gets. The opposite holds true too: If your ex-spouse claims Social Security based on your benefits, it won't have any effect on yours. Plus, neither of you can keep the other from collecting those ex-spouse benefits. In fact, your ex doesn't even need to know that you're claiming benefits based on their earnings history. If you've been married and divorced more than once, you can choose whichever Social Security benefit gives you the biggest payout (yours or any of your exes' benefits).

To avoid getting reduced retirement benefits, wait until you reach your full retirement age (FRA). While you can start getting Social Security payments at age sixty-two, the monthly check will be smaller than if you wait until *at least* your FRA to start. Your FRA is based on your birth year, and you can find that information on the Social Security website at www.ssa.gov. For example, the FRA for anyone born after 1960 is sixty-seven.

Outliving Your Ex

If your ex happens to die before you, and you meet all the Social Security criteria, you'll be eligible to get the full payment your ex was getting. This happens even if your ex had remarried; his current spouse (or other former spouses) can claim survivor benefits too.

WOMEN NEED TO CATCH UP

Ladies, Start Your Savings

Most women are woefully behind in retirement savings. That distressing fact was highlighted in the *17th Annual Transamerica Retirement Survey* of American workers and employers, which found that:

- 90 percent of women are not "very confident" that they'll be able to fully retire and live comfortably.
- 50 percent plan to work *after* they retire.
- 64 percent don't have a backup plan to cover them if they're forced to retire earlier than they want to.
- 27 percent expect to rely on Social Security as their main source of income in retirement.
- Women's median total household retirement savings is only $34,000 (estimated).

I know it sounds bleak, but you can turn this around and build up a more secure retirement nest egg. Every dollar you save today will fund your future. Smart investment choices help your money grow without taking unnecessary risks. The most important thing you can do is take action today—you'll never have more time on your side than you do right now.

YOU HAVE TO LEVEL THE PLAYING FIELD

The truth is that women face an uphill battle when it comes to saving for retirement. Overall, we earn less than men, and that affects our lifetime earnings trajectory, making it harder to save enough. Plus, those lower earnings translate into smaller Social Security benefits when we do retire.

We're also more likely to step out of our jobs to care for children or other family members (like aging parents). Leaving the workforce *for any amount of time* knocks retirement savings off track. Not only do we lose the opportunity to contribute to employer-based plans, we also lose all the growth those contributions could have earned.

On top of all that, we tend to live longer than men. Longer lives usually also mean additional healthcare costs. That means we'll need bigger nest eggs to draw from to cover that extra time.

Prioritize Retirement Savings

When you're facing a lot of current financial demands, it's easy to move "retirement savings" to the bottom of the priority list. In fact, according to a survey by global financial firm Willis Towers Watson, only 44 percent of women consider retirement savings their number one priority (compared to 60 percent of men). Overall, women ranked retirement savings as the fifth priority, trailing after things like housing costs and general savings. But consider this: If you don't start saving something toward retirement now, your future self will have no safety net and much less financial flexibility.

Because time is a key factor in retirement savings (so compounding can do the work of growing your money), it's even more important to start putting something toward it now. That's especially true if you have access to a retirement plan where your employer makes a matching contribution.

Invest (a Little) Outside Your Comfort Zone

When women invest, they tend to invest more conservatively than men, preferring to avoid risk. While that seems like a safe choice, it can actually put your financial future at greater risk. More conservative investments offer lower returns in exchange for that extra security. That means investment returns won't outpace inflation, and your nest egg will lose purchasing power.

While sticking to a conservative portfolio can be the best choice after you've retired and are looking to preserve your nest egg, taking risk in the years leading up to retirement (especially the early years) gives you the best chance of growing your money.

Talk to a Pro

Women tend to shy away from talking with financial advisors. According to a study by Fidelity Investments, 47 percent of women are hesitant to talk with a financial professional about money management and investing. Enlisting an advisor that you feel comfortable with can help you create a plan for a more secure financial future.

PILING ON THE OBSTACLES

When it comes to retirement savings, women simply face more obstacles than men do. That makes it more difficult to build up a nest egg, but not impossible. Even though it seems like current financial matters should come first, the opposite is true: Your future self desperately needs you to start saving for retirement right now. That might mean shifting priorities or redirecting a little bit of money, but it's the right choice.

Disproportionate Student Debt

Women bear the larger share of outstanding student loan debt, about two-thirds of the total. As a group, we owe close to $929 *billion*. According to a report by the American Association of University Women (AAUW):

- Women take on larger student loans than men (on average 14 percent more).
- Women earn less than men overall, so it's harder and takes longer to pay down the debt.
- Women pay more interest because the loans are larger and it takes longer to pay them off.

While it might seem like paying off the student loan faster should take priority, that strategy often ends up as a net financial loss for women. Putting money into retirement savings early on rather than paying extra on student loans helps build up the nest egg more quickly, putting more money to work for a longer time period. It's better to prioritize retirement savings even for five or ten years, and then switch priorities to focus on paying down student loans; this gives retirement savings the most time to compound.

Single Mothers Need to Save

According to the US Census, single mothers head 17.2 million households. Those women face additional barriers to saving for retirement. With constantly competing financial demands—supporting children, paying down debt, saving for college—women often shove retirement savings to the bottom of the pile. Prioritizing children and their needs doesn't mean your financial future has to be ignored.

Rather than looking for "extra" money to contribute to retirement savings, take that money off the top. Start with any amount, even if it's just $10 or $20 per paycheck, to get the savings habit started. Increase the amount periodically (at least annually, but more often is better) by just 1 or 2 percent. Any amount you put away is better than nothing—especially if you have access to a 401(k) with employer matching.

PROTECT YOUR NEST EGG

Keep Your Savings Safe

Building up a substantial retirement nest egg takes dedication and time. Protecting that nest egg takes careful planning and an intentional protection strategy. Your retirement savings faces a lot of potential threats—some you can avoid and some you cannot. Having a plan in place to address those threats before they happen will help you preserve as much of your savings as possible.

DOWN MARKETS

For people nearing retirement, anxiety over volatility in the stock market can reach unbearable levels. But as most people retire some time in their sixties, they potentially may need to support themselves for twenty or thirty years. Even people who are already retired will need to view at least a portion of their portfolios with a long-term lens. And if history is an accurate guide to the future, it's practically guaranteed that the market will tank several times during that period. That's why you need to have a plan in place to help your savings survive random market dips and dives.

Revisit Your Asset Allocation

While you were saving for retirement, your portfolio philosophy focused primarily on growth. As you near and enter retirement, it's time for a gradual shift toward preservation and income production, so you need to revisit your asset allocation strategy. Now, you want a collection of assets that can provide a retirement "paycheck" to cover your monthly expenses and still allow for some growth to give your portfolio plenty of longevity. Those safer assets could include things like bonds and annuities, along with some dividend-producing rock-solid stocks (strong companies whose stock prices *might* decline along with the market yet stand the best chance of rebounding quickly).

With a larger portion of your portfolio structured to supply enough income, the remainder can harness growth potential. The degree of growth potential and risk you can tolerate depends on a combination of your time horizon, stomach strength, and spending on "extras" (such as things like vacations and luxuries).

Diversification Softens Any Blow

Diversification is one of the most misunderstood facets of investing, and it's also one of the most important. Where asset allocation refers to the percentage of each type of asset (stocks, bonds, real estate, cash, etc.) in your portfolio, diversification is all about the different categories within each asset type. For example, if your portfolio holds 50 percent stocks, you don't want those to be all the same stock or all tech stocks or all large-cap stocks (shares in companies worth at least $5 billion); you want a broad mix of many different types of stocks. That way, if one company, industry, or market sector crashes, your entire stock portfolio won't tank. A well-diversified portfolio holds many different kinds of stocks, bonds, and real estate investments to minimize the effects of any downturn.

Don't Pull Out of the Market Entirely

The absolute worst thing you can do during a stock market crash is to sell off your stock portfolio. Doing that *guarantees* that you will lock in any losses, and remove any possibility that your portfolio could recover. Take a beat and look at your plan. If it made sense before the market went down, it still makes sense afterward. It's hard to watch your portfolio lose value, but making an emotional decision to sell can have a much worse impact. And as the Great Recession showed us, people who gritted their teeth and stayed in the market saw their portfolios recover and then enjoy explosive growth. People who pulled out of the market in 2008–2009 may never recover the value they lost.

EMERGENCY SPENDING

You can't predict when unexpected cash drains will happen, but you can be ready for them—and they will happen. Whether it's a burst pipe, a sick pet, or an adult child who's been laid off, situations that require major cash outlays will occur, often around the same time. Rather than be derailed by the financial part of any emergency that blindsides you, create a plan to deal with these blows.

Keep Your Emergency Fund in Retirement

Even after you've retired, you'll still need an emergency fund to cover unexpected expenses. Having some money stashed in an easily accessible emergency savings account lets you avoid raiding your retirement assets when a costly surprise pops up. Pulling money from your tax-deferred accounts will increase your tax bill at the end of the year (which could prompt needing to take out even more money) and reduce the potential earnings of your portfolio (decreasing how long your retirement funds will last).

Reduce the Emergency Tax Bite

To avoid the extra pain of paying the emergency expenses plus more taxes, take money from taxable accounts before pulling it out of retirement funds. You're already paying tax on those earnings anyway (such as interest and dividends), so it won't have any effect on your tax bill. If you've run out of money in regular accounts, pull from non-taxable accounts next; those withdrawals also will not increase your tax bill. Turn to your HSA (health savings account) for medical expenses or to a Roth IRA for non-medical expenses for tax-free withdrawals.

Protect Your Accounts

Retirement account theft is on the rise. Thieves target these plum accounts more often than standard investment accounts, partly because people look at them less frequently. Protect your accounts by increasing your password security, stopping paper statement delivery, *never* using public Wi-Fi, and checking your account balance regularly.

INDEX

ABOUT THE AUTHOR

Michele Cagan is a CPA, author, and financial mentor. With more than twenty years of experience, she offers unique insights into personal financial planning, from breaking out of debt and minimizing taxes, to maximizing income and building wealth. Michele has written numerous articles and books about personal finance, investing, and accounting, including *The Infographic Guide to Personal Finance, Investing 101, Stock Market 101*, and *Financial Words You Should Know*. In addition to her financial know-how, Michele has a not-so-secret love of painting, Star Wars, and chocolate. She lives in Maryland with her son, dogs, cats, and koi. Get more financial guidance from Michele by visiting SingleMomCPA.com.